PROCOPIUS

OF THE
BUILDINGS OF JUSTINIAN

Elibron Classics
www.elibron.com

Elibron Classics series.

© 2005 Adamant Media Corporation.

ISBN 1-4212-6393-9 (paperback)

This Elibron Classics Replica Edition is an unabridged facsimile of the edition published in 1888, London.

Elibron and Elibron Classics are trademarks of Adamant Media Corporation. All rights reserved.

This book is an accurate reproduction of the original. Any marks, names, colophons, imprints, logos or other symbols or identifiers that appear on or in this book, except for those of Adamant Media Corporation and BookSurge, LLC, are used only for historical reference and accuracy and are not meant to designate origin or imply any sponsorship by or license from any third party.

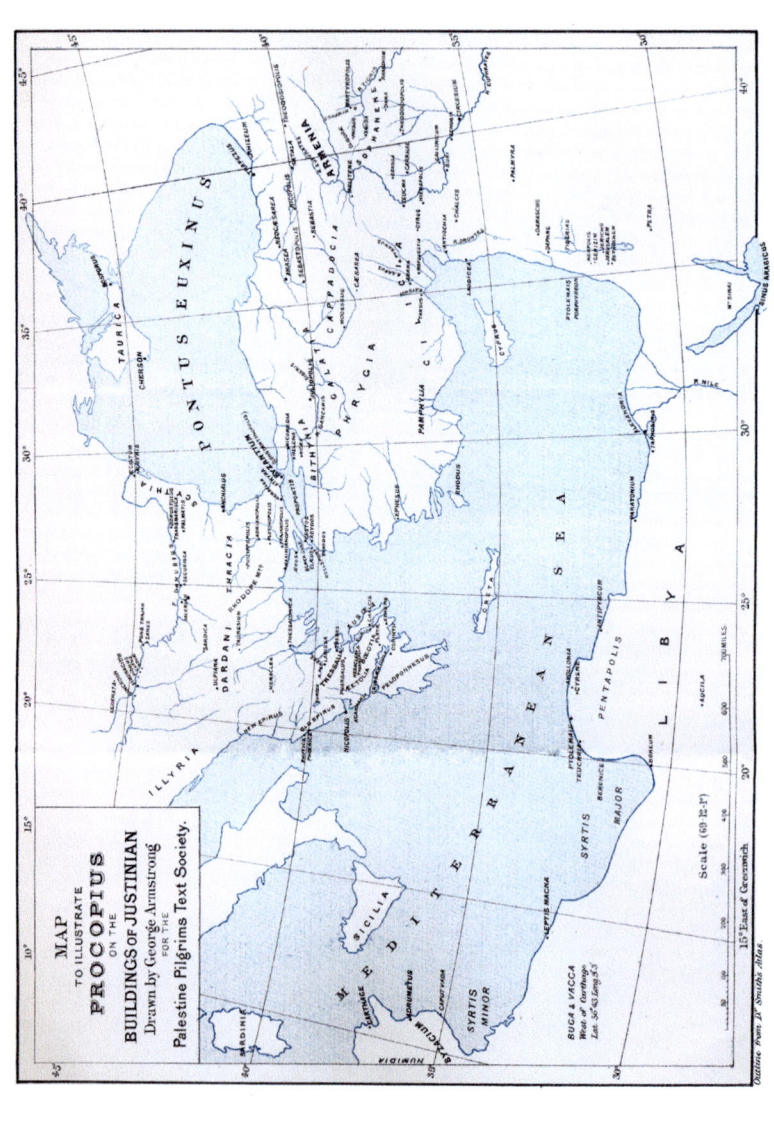

Palestine Pilgrims' Text Society.

OF THE
BUILDINGS OF JUSTINIAN.

BY

PROCOPIUS

(Circ. 560 A.D.).

Translated by
AUBREY STEWART, M.A.,
LATE FELLOW OF TRINITY COLLEGE, CAMBRIDGE,

AND ANNOTATED BY

COL. SIR C. W. WILSON, R.E., K.C.M.G., F.R.S.,

AND

PROF. HAYTER LEWIS, F.S.A.

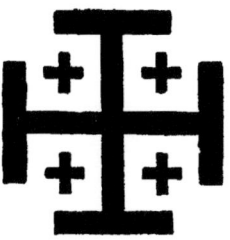

LONDON:
1. ADAM STREET, ADELPHI.
1868.

PREFACE.

PROCOPIUS was born at Cæsarea in Palestine, early in the sixth or at the end of the fifth century. He made his way, an adventurer, to Constantinople, where he began as an advocate and Professor of Rhetoric. He had the good fortune to be recommended to Belisarius, who appointed him one of his secretaries. In that capacity Procopius accompanied the general in his expedition to the East, A.D. 528, and in that against the Vandals, A.D. 533. The successful prosecution of the war enriched Belisarius to such an extent that he was enabled to maintain a retinue of 7000 men, of whom Procopius seems to have been one of the most trusted, since we find him appointed Commissary General in the Italian war. On his return to Constantinople, he was decorated with one of the innumerable titles of the Byzantine Court, and entered into the Senate. In the year 562 he was made Prefect of Constantinople, and is supposed to have died in 565—the same year as his former patron Belisarius.

His works are (1) the Histories (ἱστορίαι) in eight books, namely, two on the Persian War (408-553), two on the War with the Vandals (395-545), and four on the Wars with the Goths, bringing the History down to the year 553.

(2) The six books on the Buildings of Justinian, and (3) the *Anecdota*, or Secret History—a work which has always been attributed to him.

The 'Histories' appeared first in Latin, 1470, the translator being Leonardo Bruni d' Arezzo (Leonardo Aretino), who, believing his own MS. to be the only one in existence, gave himself out for the author. They were first published in Greek, at Augsburg, 1607; but the 'Buildings' had already appeared at Basle, 1531.

The 'Secret History' was first published, with a translation into Latin, at Lyons in 1623. The 'Histories' and the 'Anecdota' have been translated into French. An English translation of the 'Secret History' was published in 1674. No other part of Procopius has, until now, been translated.

The following version of the ' De Ædificiis ' has been specially made for the Pilgrims' Text Society, by Aubrey Stewart (late Fellow of Trinity, Cambridge), who has added the valuable notes marked (S.). The notes marked (L.), chiefly archæological, have been supplied by Professor Hayter Lewis, and those marked (W.), chiefly topographical, by Colonel Sir C. W. Wilson, the Director of the Society.

The illustrations of St. Sophia are taken from the magnificent work by Salzenberg, published at Berlin.

Those from Texier and Pullan are taken by the kind permission of Mr. Pullan from their work on ' Byzantine Architecture.'

In the investigation of the antiquities of Palestine, the name of Justinian, as associated with them, comes forward as often as that of Constantine or Herod.

From Bethlehem to Damascus—from the sea-coast to

far beyond the Jordan—there are few places of note in which some remains, dating from his era, do not exist, or in which, at the least, some records of his works are not left in the history of his time. To him Mount Sinai owes the Church of the Holy Virgin.

At Bethlehem he is said to have enlarged, if not rebuilt, the great Basilica.

At Gerizim the mountain still bears on its summit the remains of the church which he there constructed, and Tiberias is still surrounded, in part, by the walls raised by him.

He is known to have constructed a large church to the Virgin on the Mount of Olives, and several other churches in and about Jerusalem, the grandest of which is described to have been an architectural gem, was in the Harem area itself.

Besides these, which are definitely recorded to have been his work, he is supposed by some of the best authorities to have erected the Golden Gate and the Double Gate; and of late years it has been contended that the Sakhrah itself was constructed by him as it now exists.

But there is scarcely one of these edifices, where remains of them exist or are supposed so to do, which has not been the subject of controversy, the authorship of the Sakhrah (taking that as an instance) having been assigned, by various persons who would usually be considered as authorities on the subject, to the Romans under Constantine, to the Byzantines under Justinian, and to the Arabs under Abd-el-Melek.

It becomes, therefore, important to have a clear record as to what Justinian did, not only in Palestine but in other countries, so as to be able to judge to some extent, by well-authenticated examples, of the founders of those edifices whose history is involved in doubt.

Of the writers who can give us this record, none has such authority as Procopius, or gives so much detailed information; and he has, for that reason, been largely quoted by Gibbon and by well-nigh every other writer on Byzantine history; and he gives such definite information as to the dates of many of Justinian's buildings which remain to us, as to form a standard by which to recognise the general characteristics in outline and detail adopted by his architects in his greatest works, and which characterize the style now well known as Byzantine.

Its first and greatest example is St. Sofia at Constantinople, which is, perhaps, the boldest instance of a sudden change in almost every respect, whether of plan, elevation, or detail, which is known in architecture.

Before its construction, the ground-plan of well-nigh every building known to Western architects had defined the plan of all above it.

The columns in the apse of the Basilica, or church, carried galleries or other erections above it, of varied design, but in the same straight or curved lines as those beneath them.

The lines of the dome (except in slightly exceptional cases, such as the ruin known as the Temple of Minerva Medica at Rome, or the Temple of the Winds at Athens) were carried up on the distinct lines of the lower walls.

The capitals of the columns in the works of the ancient Greeks or Romans were in each building carved on the same design; and however beautiful each might be, the eye would see but one form of the Doric, Ionic, or Corinthian, through the whole range of a colonnade.

The Byzantines changed all that.

The great dome of St. Sophia (the boldest piece of novel construction ever, perhaps, attempted) forms the crown of a building quite original in plan; and this dome is placed, not as that of the Roman Pantheon, low down on thick walls of its own form, but suspended high above all the roof around it, on four arches, which spring from detached piers, the keystone alone of each arch giving a direct support to the dome; in every other part it overhangs the void in the boldest manner.

The circular work between these arches is carried in a manner which is comparatively easy to imitate now; but the rude and often picturesque results of attempts at imitation in mediæval times, more especially in the South of France, show how difficult the work was found to be at the outset.

Earthquake and faults of construction occasioned the rebuilding of the great dome; but it still crowns, after a trial of more than 1,300 years, one of the most beautiful buildings in existence.

Then the capitals of the columns, whose general outlines bear few traces of the ancient orders, were often carved each in a different manner, and, though harmonizing with each other in general outline, could bear separate scrutiny, and show each a special motive and design.

The carving of these capitals, and of the other beautiful scroll-work and foliage which decorate the walls of St. Sophia, has come down to us through the Normans, and is quite peculiar.

It had none of the soft, round forms which the Romans loved, but is cut in a sharp, crisp, and somewhat stiff style, casting distinctly marked and sharp shadows, and the eyes of the foliage and other well-marked parts are emphasized by being deeply drilled in. Many of the Byzantine characteristics had been, to a large extent, foreshadowed in Eastern buildings, even at so early a time as the Assyrian bas-reliefs; but it is to Byzantine architects, under the fostering care of Justinian, that we owe the picturesque changes and details of that style, the Byzantine, which takes its name from his capital and is, to a large extent, identified with himself.

All the drawings have been made for this volume by Mr. George Armstrong, formerly on the Survey Party under Captain Conder and Captain Kitchener.

(L.)

LIST OF PLATES.

	PAGE
MAP ILLUSTRATING PROCOPIUS	*Frontispiece*
PLAN OF CONSTANTINOPLE	1
CHURCH OF ST. SOPHIA	5
DETAILS OF CAPITALS, ETC., OF ST. SOPHIA	7
SECTION OF ST. SOPHIA	9
SS. SERGIUS AND BACCHUS, CHURCH OF	19
FORTIFICATIONS AT DARA	42
CASTLE AND COLUMNS OF EDESSA	60
CISTERN OF IMBAHER OR BATHS OF ANTONINUS	132
BRIDGE ACROSS THE RIVER SANGARIS	133
ES SAKHRA (DOME OF THE ROCK)	139
EL AKSA	140
CHURCH ON MOUNT GERIZIM	144
CHURCH AT BETHLEHEM	148
CHURCH OF MAGNE KAHIREH	160

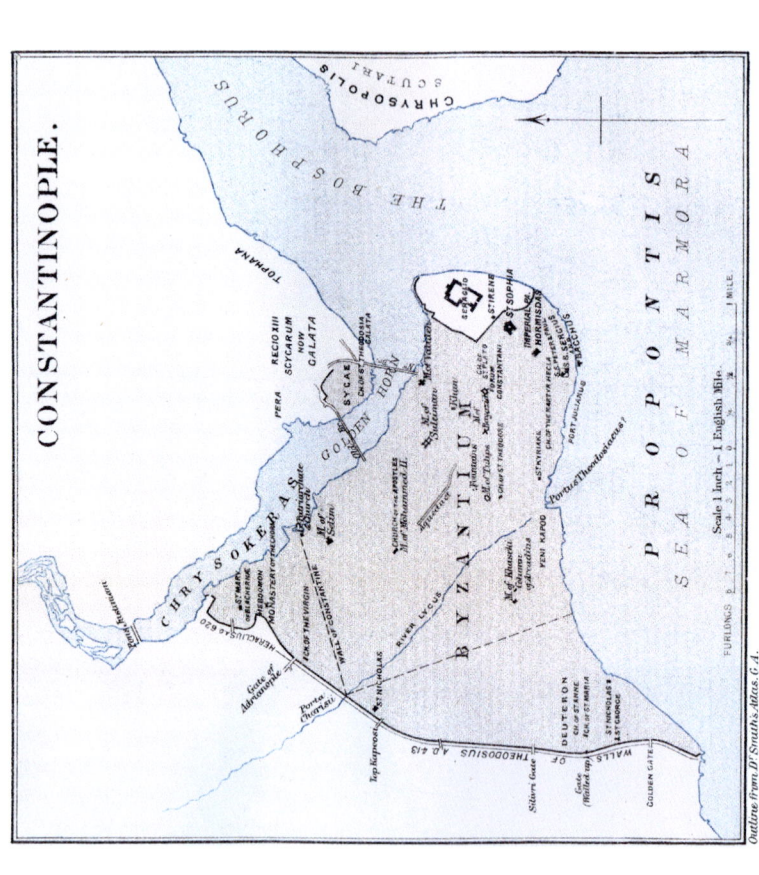

THE
SIX BOOKS OF PROCOPIUS OF CÆSAREA,

ON THE

BUILDINGS OF THE LORD JUSTINIAN.

INTRODUCTION.

I HAVE not begun this work through any desire to make a display of my own virtue, or trusting to my powers of language, or wishing to gain credit by my knowledge of the places described, for I had nothing to encourage me to undertake so bold a project. But I have often reflected on the great blessings which countries derive from history, which transmits to posterity the remembrance of our ancestors, and opposes the efforts of time to cover them with oblivion ; which always encourages virtue in its readers by its praise, and deters them from vice by its blame, and in this way destroys its power. All we need study then is to make clear what has been done, and by whom of mankind it was done; and this, I imagine, is not impossible even for the weakest and feeblest writer; besides this, the writing of history enables subjects who have been kindly treated by their rulers, to express their gratitude, and to make a more than adequate return, seeing that they only for a time enjoy the goodness of their princes, while they render their virtues immortal in the memory of their descendants, many of whom in this very way have been led by the glory of their ancestors to a love of virtue, and have been probably preserved from a dissolute course of life by the dread of disgrace. I will shortly explain my object in making these prefatory remarks.

The Emperor Justinian was born in our time,* and succeeding to the throne when the state was decayed, added greatly to its extent and glory by driving out from it the barbarians, who for so long a time had forced their way into it, as I have briefly narrated in my 'History of the Wars.' They say that Themistocles, the son of Neocles, prided himself on his power of making a small state great, but our Emperor has the power of adding other states to his own, for he has annexed to the Roman Empire many other states which at his accession were independent, and has founded innumerable cities which had no previous existence. As for religion, which he found uncertain and torn by various heresies, he destroyed everything which could lead to error, and securely established the true faith upon one solid foundation. Moreover, finding the laws obscure through their unnecessary multitude, and confused by their conflict with one another, he firmly established them by reducing the number of those which were unnecessary, and in the case of those that were contradictory, by confirming the better ones. He forgave of his own accord those who plotted against him,

---

* 'A new era for Christian architecture commenced with his reign. The historian Procopius has simplified, in the different provinces of his Eastern empire, the task to those who would search for vestiges of buildings erected by this Prince. Anthemius was selected by him as his architect, and the Church of St. Sophia became the type of all the Greek churches from the sixth century. The basilica was, until his time, the type of the Christian church. Anthemius abandoned this form. The chief feature of the church was the dome, the form of the oblong nave being abandoned.'—Texier and Pullan, 'Byzantine Architecture' (fol., London, 1864), p. 20. (L.)

and, by loading with wealth those who were in want, and relieving them from the misfortunes which had afflicted them, he rendered the empire stable and its members happy. By increasing his armies he strengthened the Roman Empire, which lay everywhere exposed to the attacks of barbarians, and fortified its entire frontier by building strong places. Of his other acts the greater part have been described by me in other works, but his great achievements in building are set forth in this book. We learn from tradition that Cyrus the Persian was a great king, and the chief founder of the empire of his countrymen; but whether he had any resemblance to that Cyrus who is described by Xenophon the Athenian in his Cyropædia, I have no means of telling, for possibly the art of the writer has given some embellishments to his achievements; while as for our present Emperor Justinian (whom I think one may rightly call a king by nature, since, as Homer says, he is as gentle as a father), if one accurately considers his empire, one will regard that of Cyrus as mere child's play.* The proof of this will be that the empire, as I just now said, has been more than doubled by him, both in extent and in power; whilst his royal clemency is proved by the fact that those who wickedly plotted against his life, although they were clearly convicted, not only are alive and in possession of their property at the present day, but even command Roman armies, and have been promoted to the consular dignity. Now, as I said before, we must turn our attention to the buildings of this monarch, lest posterity, beholding the enormous size and number of them, should deny their being the work of one man; for the works of many men of former times, not being confirmed by history, have

---

* There is a pun in the original upon παιδιά and παιδεία. Cf. Gibbon, ch. xl. (S.)

been disbelieved through their own excessive greatness. As is natural, the foundation of all my account will be the buildings in Byzantium, for, as the old proverb has it, when we begin a work we ought to put a brilliant frontispiece to it.

CHURCH OF ST SOPHIA.
HALF SECTION THROUGH GREAT DOME AND TRANSEPT

BOOK I.

I. The lowest dregs of the people in Byzantium once assailed the Emperor Justinian in the rebellion called Nika, which I have clearly described in my 'History of the Wars.' To prove that it was not merely against the Emperor, but no less against God that they took up arms, they ventured to burn the church of the Christians. (This church the people of Byzantium call Sophia, *i.e.*, Σοφία—*Wisdom;* a name most worthy of God.) God permitted them to effect this crime, knowing how great the beauty of this church would be when restored. Thus the church was entirely reduced to ashes; but the Emperor Justinian not long afterwards adorned it in such a fashion, that if anyone had asked the Christians in former times if they wished their church to be destroyed and thus restored, showing them the appearance of the church which we now see, I think it probable that they would have prayed that they might as soon as possible behold their church destroyed, in order that it might be turned into its present form. The Emperor, regardless of expense of all kinds, pressed on its restoration, and collected together all the workmen from every land. Anthemius of Tralles,*

---

* 'Taken altogether, there is no building erected during the first thirteen centuries after the Christian era which, as an interior, is either so beautiful or so worthy of attentive study as this.'—Fergusson, 'Handbook of Architecture' (8vo., London, 1855), p. 951. (L.)

In addition to Procopius, the erection of St. Sophia has been described by Agathias, and at much greater length by Paulus Silentiarius, and the three descriptions have been compared and analyzed in the 'Corpus Historiæ Byzantinæ,' *s.v.* Paulus Silentiarius. (L.)

A full description of St. Sophia with plans sections, and detailed

by far the most celebrated architect, not only of his own but of all former times, carried out the King's zealous intentions, organized the labours of the workmen, and prepared models of the future construction. Associated with him was another architect named Isidorus, a Milesian by birth, a man of intelligence, and worthy to carry out the plans of the Emperor Justinian. It is, indeed, a proof of the esteem with which God regarded the Emperor, that He furnished him with men who would be so useful in effecting his designs, and we are compelled to admire the intelligence of the Emperor, in being able to choose the most suitable of mankind to carry out the noblest of his works.

The church consequently presented a most glorious spectacle, extraordinary to those who beheld it, and altogether incredible to those who are told of it. In height it rises to the very heavens, and overtops the neighbouring buildings like a ship anchored among them: it rises above the rest of the city, which it adorns, while it forms a part of it, and it is one of its beauties that being a part of the city, and growing out of it, it stands so high above it, that from it the whole city can be beheld as from a watch-tower. Its length and breadth are so judiciously arranged that it appears to be both long and wide without being disproportioned. It is distinguished by indescribable beauty, for it excels both in its size and in the harmony of its proportion, having no part excessive and none deficient; being more magnificent than ordinary buildings, and much more elegant than those which are out of proportion. It is singularly full of light and sunshine; you would declare that the place is not lighted by the sun from without, but that the rays are produced within itself, such an abundance of light is poured into this church. Now the front of the church (that is to say the part towards the rising

---

drawings of the mosaics, sculpture, etc., is given by Salzenburg in his splendid work 'Alt Christliche von Constantinopel' (Berlin, 1854). (L.)

CHURCH OF ST SOPHIA.
DETAILS OF ORNAMENTAL WORK

sun, where the sacred mysteries are performed in honour

Specimen of Details of Capitals &c of St Sophia. From Salzenburgi.

of God) is built as follows. The building rises from the ground, not in a straight line, but set back somewhat obliquely, and retreating in the middle into the form of a half-circle, a form which those who are learned in these matters call semi-cylindrical,

rising perpendicularly. The upper part of this work ends in the fourth part of a sphere, and above it another crescent-shaped structure is raised upon the adjacent parts of the building, admirable for its beauty, but causing terror by the apparent weakness of its construction; for it appears not to rest upon a secure foundation, but to hang dangerously over the heads of those within, although it is really supported with especial firmness and safety. On each side of these there are columns standing

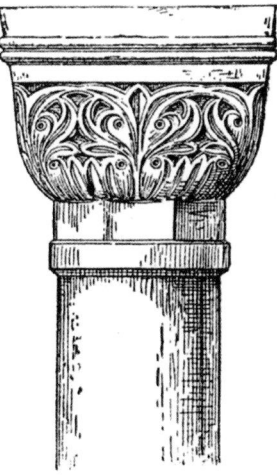

upon the floor, which themselves also are not placed in a straight line, but arranged with an inward curve of semicircular shape, one beyond another, like the dancers in a chorus. These columns support above them a crescent-shaped structure. Opposite this east wall is built another wall containing the entrances, and upon either side of it also stand columns with stonework above them in a half-circle exactly like those previously described. In the midst of the church are four masses of stone called piers, two on the north and two on the south side, opposite and equal to one another, having four columns in the central space between each. These piers are composed of large stones fitted together, the stones being carefully selected and cleverly jointed into one another by the masons, reaching to a great height. Looking at them you would compare them to perpendicular cliffs. Upon these four arches rise in a quadrilateral form. The extremities of these arches join one another in pairs, and rest at their ends upon these piers, while the other part of them rise to a great height, and are suspended in the air. Two of these arches, that is, those towards the rising and the setting sun, are constructed over the empty air, but the remainder have under them some stonework, with small columns. Now above these arches is raised a circular building of a spherical form through which the light of day first shines; for the building, I imagine, overtops the whole country, and has small openings left on purpose, so that the places where these intervals in the construction occur may serve for conductors of light. Thus far I imagine the building is not incapable of being described, even by a weak and feeble tongue. As the arches are arranged in a quadrangular figure, the stonework between them takes the shape of a triangle; the lower angle of each triangle,

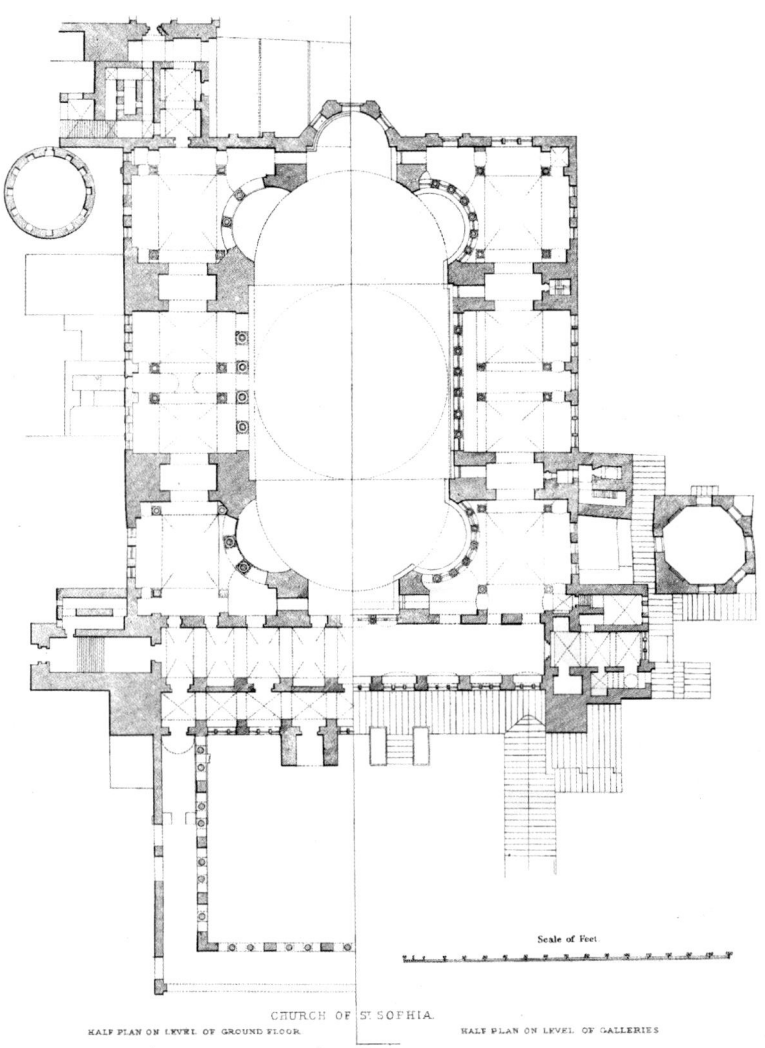

CHURCH OF ST SOPHIA.

HALF PLAN ON LEVEL OF GROUND FLOOR.   HALF PLAN ON LEVEL OF GALLERIES.

being compressed between the shoulders of the arches, is slender, while the upper part becomes wider as it rises in the space between them, and ends against the circle which rises from thence, forming there its remaining angles. A spherical-shaped dome standing upon this circle makes it exceedingly beautiful; from the lightness of the building it does not appear to rest upon a solid foundation, but to cover the place beneath as though it were suspended from heaven by the fabled golden chain. All these parts surprisingly joined to one another in the air, suspended one from another, and resting only on that which is next to them, form the work into one admirably harmonious whole, which spectators do not care to dwell upon for long in the mass, as each individual part attracts the eye and turns it to itself. The sight causes men to constantly change their point of view, and the spectator can nowhere point to any part which he admires more than the rest, but having viewed the art which appears everywhere, men contract their eyebrows as they look at each point, and are unable to comprehend such workmanship, but always depart thence stupified through their incapacity to comprehend it. So much for this.

The Emperor Justinian and the architects Anthemius and Isidorus used many devices to construct so lofty a church with security. One alone of these I will at this present time explain, by which a man may form some opinion of the strength of the whole work; as for the others, I am not able to discover them all, and find it impossible to explain them in words. It is as follows:—The piers[*] of

---

[*] 'The solid piles which sustained the cupola were composed of huge blocks of freestone, hewn into squares and triangles, fortified by circles of iron, and firmly cemented by the infusion of lead and quicklime.'—Gibbon, ch. xl. (S.)

which I just now spoke are not constructed in the same manner as the rest of the building, but in this fashion: they consist of quadrangular courses of stones, rough by nature, but made smooth by art; of these stones, those which make the projecting angles of the pier are cut angularly, while those which go in the middle parts of the sides are cut square. They are fastened together not with what is called unslaked lime, not with bitumen, the boast of Semiramis at Babylon, nor anything of the kind, but with lead, which is poured between the interstices, and which, pervading the whole structure, has sunk into the joints of the stones, and binds them together; this is how they are built. Let us now proceed to describe the remaining parts of the church. The entire ceiling is covered with pure gold, which adds glory to its beauty, though the rays of light reflected upon the gold from the marble surpass it in beauty; there are two porticos on each side, which do not in any way dwarf the size of the church, but add to its width. In length they reach quite to the ends, but in height they fall short of it; these also have a domed ceiling and are adorned with gold. Of these two porticos, the one is set apart for male, and the other for female worshippers; there is no variety in them, nor do they differ in any respect from one another, but their very equality and similarity add to the beauty of the church. Who could describe the galleries* of the portion set apart for women, or the numerous porticos and cloistered courts

---

* 'Nine western doors open into the vestibule, and from thence into the *narthex* or exterior portico. That portico was the humble station of the penitents. The nave, or body of the church, was filled by the congregation of the faithful; but the two sexes were prudently distinguished, and the upper and lower galleries were allotted for the more private devotion of the women.'—Gibbon, ch. xl. (S.)

with which the church is surrounded? who could tell of the beauty of the columns and marbles with which the church is adorned? one would think that one had come upon a meadow full of flowers in bloom: who would not admire the purple tints of some and the green of others, the glowing red and glittering white, and those, too, which nature, like a painter, has marked with the strongest contrasts of colour? Whoever enters there to worship perceives at once that it is not by any human strength or skill, but by the favour of God that this work has been perfected; his mind rises sublime to commune with God, feeling that He cannot be far off, but must especially love to dwell in the place which He has chosen; and this takes place not only when a man sees it for the first time, but it always makes the same impression upon him, as though he had never beheld it before. No one ever became weary of this spectacle, but those who are in the Church delight in what they see, and, when they leave it, magnify it in their talk about it; moreover, it is impossible accurately to describe the treasure of gold and silver plate and gems, which the Emperor Justinian has presented to it; but by the description of one of them, I leave the rest to be inferred. That part of the church which is especially sacred, and where the priests alone are allowed to enter, which is called the Sanctuary, contains forty thousand pounds' weight of silver.

The above is an account, written in the most abridged and cursory manner, describing in the fewest possible words the most admirable structure of the church at Constantinople which is called the Great Church, built by the Emperor Justinian, who did not merely supply the funds for it, but assisted it by the labour and powers of his mind, as I will now explain. Of the two arches which I lately mentioned (the architects call them 'lori'*), that one which stands towards the east had been built up on each side, but had not altogether been completed in the middle, where it was still imperfect; now the piers upon which the building rested, unable to support the weight which was put upon them, somehow all at once split open, and seemed as though before long they would fall to pieces. Upon this Anthemius and Isidorus, terrified at what had taken place, referred the matter to the Emperor, losing all confidence in their own skill. He at once, I know not by what impulse, but probably inspired by heaven, for he is not an architect, ordered them to carry round this arch; for it, said he, resting upon itself, will no longer need the piers below. Now if this story were unsupported by witnesses, I am well assured that it would seem to be written in order to flatter, and to be quite incredible; but as there are many witnesses now alive of what then took place, I shall not hesitate to finish it. The workmen performed his bidding, the arch was safely suspended, and proved by experiment the truth of his conception. So much then for this part of the building; now with regard to the other arches, those looking to the south and to the north, the following incidents took place. When the arches called 'lori' were raised aloft during the building of the church, everything below them laboured under their

---

* Λώρους. I am unacquainted with the precise meaning of this word. Ducange, in his 'Glossary,' describes ΛΩΡΟΣ as 'Fornix,' 'arcus,' Ἀψίς, quoting Procopius. But this gives no definite information; nor, after consulting with several well-known authorities on this subject, can I find that the application of the term is now known. It is not alluded to either in Britton's 'Dictionary,' or Willis's 'Nomenclature of the Middle Ages.' From the context and Ducange's use of the word ἄψις, I presume that λῶρος is applied to the great arch forming the opening of an apse. (L.)

weight, and the columns which are placed there shed little scales, as though they had been planed. Alarmed at this, the architects again referred the matter to the Emperor, who devised the following plan. He ordered the upper part of the work that was giving way, where it touched the arches, to be taken down for the present, and to be replaced long afterwards when the damp had thoroughly left the fabric. This was done, and the building has stood safely afterwards, so that the structure as it were bears witness to the Emperor.

II. In front of the Senate House there is an open place which the people of Constantinople call the Augustaeum : in it there are are not less than seven courses of stone in a quadrangular form, arranged like steps, each one so much less in extent than that which is below, that each one of the stones projects sufficiently for the men who frequent that place to sit upon them as upon steps. From the topmost course a column rises to a great height—not a monolith, but composed of stones of a considerable periphery, which are cut square, and are fitted into one another by the skill of the masons. The finest brass, cast into panels and garlands, surrounds these stones on every side, binding them firmly together, while it covers them with ornament, and in all parts, especially at the capital and the base, imitates the form of the column. This brass is in colour paler than unalloyed gold; and its value is not much short of its own weight in silver. On the summit of the column there stands an enormous horse, with his face turned towards the east—a noble sight. He appears to be walking, and proceeding swiftly forwards ; he raises his left fore-foot as though to tread upon the earth before him, while the other rests upon the stone beneath it, as though it would make the next step, while he places his hind feet together, so that they may be ready when he bids them move. Upon this horse sits a colossal brass figure of the Emperor, habited as Achilles, for so his costume is called; he wears hunting-shoes, and his ankles are not covered by his greaves. He wears a corslet like an ancient hero, his head is covered by a helmet which seems to nod, and a plume glitters upon it. A poet would say that it was that 'star of the dog-days' mentioned in Homer.* He looks towards the east, directing his course, I imagine, against the Persians; in his left hand he holds a globe, by which the sculptor signifies that all lands and seas are subject to him. He holds no sword or spear, or any other weapon, but a cross stands upon the globe, through which he has obtained his empire and victory in war; he stretches forward his right hand towards the east, and spreading out his fingers seems to bid the barbarians in that quarter to remain at home and come no further. This is the appearance of the statue.

The Church of Irene,† which was next to the great

---

* Hom. Il., xxii. 27. (S.)

† 'St. Irene templum a Constantino M. extructum—tres sacras ædes. Deiparæ scilicet, St. Theodori et St. Irenes, eidem magnæ ecclesiæ unitas fuisse, neque proprium clerum habuisse, qui in iis sacra ministeria perageret.' 'Unde cum Sophianæ ædis appendix fuerit, intra ejusdem septa ædificata dicitur.' 'Denique concussa est ipsa ædes eo terræ motu qui accidit Leone Isauro regnante. Hodie intra septum regium includi.'—Ducange, ' Byzantinæ Historiæ Scriptoribus Constantinopolis Christiana' (Venice, fol., 1729), lib. iv., p. 102.

Rebuilt, in part at all events, by Justinian late in his reign, but in a style entirely different from that of St. Sophia or SS. Sergius and Bacchus, being oblong on plan, with aisles and an apse at the east end. This apse was cleared in 1881. Mr. Edwin Freshfield, who visited the church at that time, states that he 'found that it was filled with marble benches, or steps, somewhat similar to the Church of Torcello, near Venice. There is no doubt that they formed part of the original arrangement of the church, and that this was due to its being the Patriarchal church.'—*Athenæum*, 15th August, 1885. (L.)

church, and was burnt down together with it, was rebuilt on a large scale by the Emperor Justinian—a church scarcely second to any in Byzantium except that of Sophia. There was between these two churches a hospice for the relief of destitute persons and those in the last extremity of disease, suffering in body as well as in fortune, which was built in former times by a God-fearing man named Sampson. This also did not remain unscathed by the insurgents, but perished in the fire, together with the two neighbouring churches. The Emperor Justinian rebuilt it in a more magnificent fashion, and with a much greater number of rooms, and he has also endowed it with a great annual revenue, in order that the sufferings of more unfortunate men may be relieved in it for the future. Insatiate as he was in his love for God, he built two other hospices opposite to this, in what are called the houses of Isidorus and Arcadius, being assisted in these pious works by the Empress Theodora. As for all the other churches which this Emperor raised in honour of Christ, they are so many in number and so great in size that it is impossible to describe them in detail, for no power of words nor one's whole life would suffice to collect and to recite the list of their several names: let this much suffice.

III. We must begin with the churches of the Virgin Mary, for it is understood that this is the wish of the Emperor himself, and the true method of description distinctly points out that from God we ought to proceed to the Mother of God. The Emperor Justinian built in all parts of the Roman empire many churches dedicated to the Virgin, so magnificent and large, and constructed with such a lavish expenditure of money, that a person beholding any one of them singly would imagine it to have been his only work, and that he had spent the whole period of his reign in adorning it alone. For the present, as I said before, I shall describe the churches in Byzantium. One of the churches of the Virgin* was built by him outside the walls, in a place named Blachernæ (for he must be credited with the pious foundations of Justin, his uncle, since he administered his kingdom at his own discretion). This church is near the sea-shore, of great sanctity and magnificence; it is long, yet its width is well proportioned to its length, and above and below it is supported and rests on nothing less than sections of Parian marble which stand in the form of columns. These columns are arranged in a straight line in all parts of the church except in the middle, where they are set back. Those who enter this church especially admire its lofty and at the same time secure construction, and its splendid yet not meretricious beauty.

He built another church in her honour in the place which is called the Fountain, where there is a thick grove of cypress trees, a meadow whose rich earth blooms with flowers, a garden abounding in fruit, a fountain which noiselessly pours forth a quiet and sweet stream of water, in short where all the surroundings beseem a sacred place. Such is the country around the church; but as for the church itself, it is not easy to describe it in fitting words, to form an idea of it in the mind, or to express it in language; let it suffice for me to say thus much of it, that in beauty and size it surpasses most other churches. Both these churches are built outside the city walls, the one at the place where the wall starts from the sea-shore,

---

* *Ædes sacræ Deiparæ dicatæ. Deiparæ Blachernarum.* Ædem vero Deiparæ Blachernianam a Pulcheria Augusta primum ædificatam scribunt passim scriptores Byzantini. Hanc postmodum de novo instauravit Justinus senior (V. Procopius de Ædifs., lib. i., c. iii.). Denique solo tenus incensum fuisse sub Romano Diogene, restauratum postmodum, novis ornamentis et nova ædificiorum accessione auxit mire Andronicus senior.—Ducange, lib. iv., pp. 55, 56. (L.)

the latter close to what is called the Golden Gate, which is near the further end of the fortifications, in order that both of them might form impregnable defences for the city walls. Besides these, in the temple of Hera, now called the Hiereum, he erected a church in honour of the Virgin, which cannot easily be described.

In that part of the city which is called Deuteron* he built a noble and admirable church in honour of St. Anne, whom some think to have been the mother of the Virgin, and the grandmother of Christ; for God, in choosing to become man, subjected Himself to having grand-parents and a genealogy on His mother's side like a man. Not very far from this church, in the last street of the city, there is a fine church built in honour of the martyr Zoe.

He found the church of the Archangel Michael† at Byzantium small, very dark, and quite unworthy of being dedicated to the archangel, having been built by one Senator, a patrician in former times, and in shape very like a small bedroom in a poor man's house. Wherefore he razed it entirely to the ground, that no part of its former unseemliness might be left, and rebuilding it of a goodly size, in the manner which we now see, changed it into a building

* 'Deuterum, Δεύτερον, locus et tractus urbis ita appellatus occurrit sæpe apud scriptores Byzantinos qui in eo ædes sacras Stæ. Annæ, Sti. Georgii, St. Pauli et SS. Notariorum extitisse narrant.—Procopius scribens haud procul a St. Annæ æde in Deutero aliam ædificasse Justinianum Zoæ Martyri, ad ultimam urbis plateam.—Porro Deuterum dictum fuisse, quod secundo milliari a vetere Byzantio dissitum esset.' —Ducange, lib. ii., p. 133. (L.)

† 'Templum quod Αρχαγγέλων et τὰ Στείρου appellatum fuit, id nominis sortitum eit, a Patricia quadam sterili, Leone M. Impr. Quum autem esset parvum oratorium ampliorem ædem ibi excitavit Judinianus M. quam terræ motu collapsam instauravit Basilius Macedo, qui insuper ablatam ex Strategio Phialam æream illuc transposuit. Observat porro Maltratus in margine Procopii περὶ τοῦ ναοῦ τοῦ αὐτομάτου ἐν τῷ Σενατορίῳ—unde colligitur regionem in qua hæc ædes extructa fuit senatorii nomine donatam.'—Ducange, lib. iv., p. 66. (S.)

of wonderful beauty. This church is of a quadrangular form, its length apparently not greatly exceeding its width; of its sides, that which looks towards the east has at its extremities a thick wall constructed of a great mass of stones, but in the middle is set back, forming a recess, on each side of which the roof is supported by columns of variegated stone. The opposite wall, that towards the west, is pierced with doors opening into the church.

IV. His faith in the Apostles of Christ is testified in the following manner: In the first place he built the Church to SS. Peter and Paul, which did not exist before in Byzantium, close to the King's palace, which was formerly called by the name of Hormisdas.* This was once his own private house; and when he became Emperor of the Romans, he made it look worthy of a palace by the magnificence of its buildings, and joined it to the other imperial apartments. Here also he built another church dedicated to the glorious saints Sergius and Bacchus,† and

* 'Assumptus ille in Hormisdæ SS. Sergii et Bacchi Monasterio quod Palatio adjacet.'—Ducange, lib. iv., p. 93.

† 'Juxta Hormisdæ palatium, ubi priusquam imperium adeptus esset habitabat Justinianus. Hormisdæ monasterium nuncupatur. Quippe ad Hormisdæ palatium, quod Imperator factus magno Palatio adjunxit, bina excitavit templa, quæ a latere cohærebant, et vestibulorum porticus, atria et propylea communia habebant. Cumque pari invicem decore ac magnitudine essent, in hoc tamen differebant, quod hujus directa esset longitudo, illius vero columnæ in semicirculum dispositæ essent fere omnes, priorem ædem SS. Petro et SS. Paulo, alteram SS. Sergio et Baccho dicavit.'—Ducange, lib. iv., p. 93. (L.)

One of the most interesting buildings in Constantinople. It is rightly called the Little Agia Sofia, as it was the first essay of Justinian, before he became Emperor, in the style of which the Great Church was to be the glory. I make no doubt that Anthemius of Tralles was the architect, and the building has in it many of the peculiarities of the Church Agia Sofia. It is further interesting as having furnished the model for the Church of St. Vitale at Ravenna, some of the details in the latter church being also copied from the Kutchuk Agia Sofia. This church was dedicated to SS. Sergius and Bacchus.—Mr. Edwin Freshfield, in *Athenæum*, August 15, 1885, p. 217. (L.)

afterwards another church standing obliquely to it. These two churches stand, not facing one another, but obliquely towards one another, joined together, and vying one with another. They have a common entrance, are equal to one another in all respects, are surrounded by a

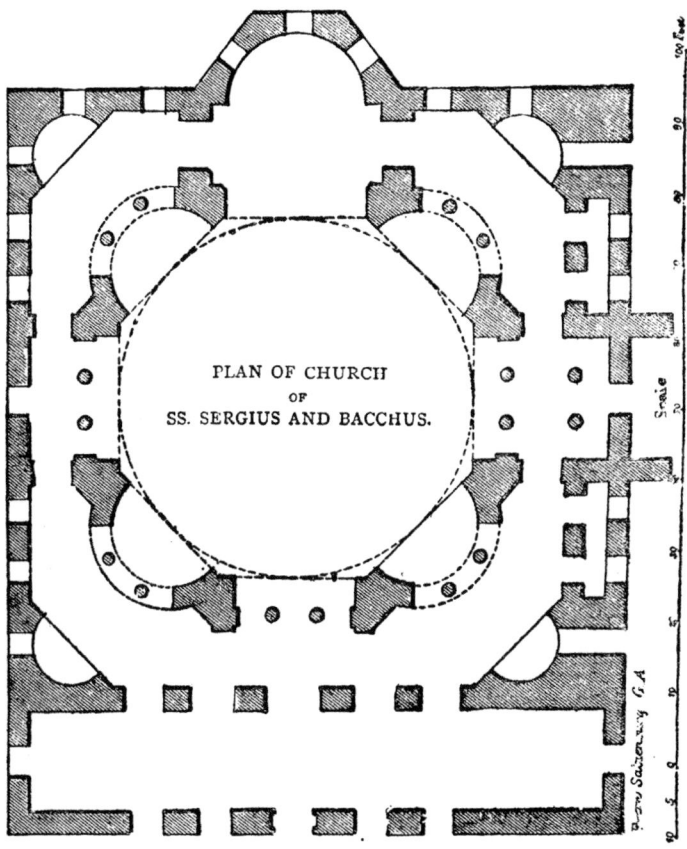

boundary wall, and neither of them exceeds the other or falls short of it, either in beauty, size, or any other respect; for each alike reflects the rays of the sun from its polished marble, and is alike covered with lavish gilding and adorned with offerings; in one respect alone they differ, that the length of one is straight, whereas the columns of the other for the most part stand in a semicircle. They both have one portico at their vestibule, which from its great length is called Narthex.* The whole vestibule, the court, the inner doors from the court and the neighbourhood of the palace are alike common to both, and both these churches are so admirable that they form a great ornament to the entire city, and especially to the palace.

After this, out of his exceeding great reverence for all the Apostles,† he did as follows. In ancient times there was one church at Byzantium dedicated to all the Apostles, but through length of time it had become ruinous, and seemed not likely to stand much longer. Justinian took this entirely down, and was careful not only to rebuild it, but to render it more admirable both in size and beauty; he carried out his intention in the following manner. Two lines were drawn in the form of a cross, joining one another in the middle, the upright one pointing to the rising and setting sun, and the other cross line towards the north and the south wind. These were surrounded by a circuit of walls,

---

* νάρθηξ = a reed. (S.)

† 'Sanctorum apostolorum templum, omnium quæ in urbe extiterunt, post Sophianum celeberrimum et pulcherrimum extruxit Constantinus Magnus, ut in eo Imperatores Christiani post obitum humarentur.'— V. Eusebius, lib. iv., de Vita Consti., c. 58; Ducange, lib. iv., p. 71.

Constantine erected it. The walls were covered with marble from pavement to roof; the nave was ceiled, and the dome, as well as the roof, was covered with plates of brass. Constantine caused his tomb to be erected in the centre of the church. It was damaged by an earthquake soon after its erection, but was repaired by Justinian.— Texier and Pullan, p. 12.

In 1038 A.D., the Church of the Apostles suffered terribly in an earthquake, and was pulled down by Mohammed II.—Texier and Pullan, 'Byzantine Architecture,' fol. 1864, p. 161. (L.)

and within by columns placed both above and below; at the crossing of the two straight lines, that is, about the middle point of them, there is a place set apart, which may not be entered except by the priests, and which is consequently termed the Sanctuary. The transepts which lie on each side of this, about the cross line, are of equal length; but that part of the upright line towards the setting sun is built so much longer than the other part as to form the figure of the cross. That part of the roof which is above the Sanctuary is constructed like the middle part of the Church of Sophia, except that it yields to it in size; for the four arches are suspended and connected with one another in the same fashion, the circular building standing above them is pierced with windows, and the spherical dome which overarches it seems to be suspended in the air, and not to stand upon a firm base, although it is perfectly secure. In this manner the middle part of the roof is built: now the roof over the four limbs of the church is constructed of the same size as that which I have described over the middle, with this one exception, that the wall underneath the spherical part is not pierced with windows. When he had completed the building of this Sanctuary, the Apostles made it evident to all that they were pleased and thoroughly delighted with the honour paid them by the Emperor; for the bodies of the Apostles Andrew, Luke, and Timothy, which had before this been invisible and altogether unknown, were then made manifest to all men, signifying, I imagine, that they did not reject the faith of the Emperor, but permitted him openly to behold them, to approach and to touch them, that he might gain from them assistance and security for his life. This was discovered in the following manner.

The Emperor Constantine built this church in the

name and in honour of the Apostles, making a decree that there should be a sepulchre there for himself, and for those who should rule after him, women as well as men; which is observed even to the present day. Here also the body of the father of Constantine was laid; but he did not in any way hint that the bodies of the Apostles were there, nor did there appear to be any place set apart for the bodies of saints. When, however, the Emperor Justinian was rebuilding this church, the workmen dug up the whole foundation, lest any unseemly thing should be left in it. They saw there three neglected wooden coffins, which declared by inscriptions upon them that they contained the bodies of the Apostles Andrew, Luke, and Timothy, which the Emperor and all Christian men beheld with the greatest delight. A solemn procession and public festival was ordered, and, after the customary rites had been performed in their honour, the coffins were covered up, and again placed in the ground. The place was not left unmarked or uncared for, but was reverently dedicated to the bodies of the Apostles. In return for the respect paid them by the Emperor, the Apostles, as I said before, made themselves manifest to all men; for, under a religious prince, the host of heaven do not hold themselves aloof from the affairs of men, but love to mingle with them, and rejoice in intercourse with mankind.

Who could be silent about the Church of Acacius,* which, being ruinous, he pulled down and built up again from its very foundations, adding wonderfully to its size?

---

* 'S. Acacii qui martyrium passus est Byzantii sub Diocletiano, ædem ædificavit in Heptascalo Constantinus Magnus. Ædis situm eundem designant Menæa, ad 4 Junii. Ecclesiam S. Acacii conditam quidem a Constantino Magno, sed illius nomen ædi primum imposuisse Justinianum. Justinianus autem hanc a fundamentis instauravit, disjecta priore æde. Denique cum rursum ruinam minaretur de novo instauratum est a Basilio Macedone.'—Ducange, lib. iv., pp. 80, 81. (L.)

It rests on all sides upon brilliantly white columns, and its floor is covered with similar marble, from which so bright a light is reflected as to make one imagine that the whole church is covered with snow. Two porticos stand in front of it, the one supported on columns, and the other looking towards the forum. I was within a little of omitting to mention the church which was dedicated to St. Plato the Martyr,* a truly worthy and noble building, not far from the forum, which is named after the Emperor Constantine; and likewise the church dedicated to the Martyr Mocius,† which is the largest of all these churches. Besides this, there is the Church of the Martyr Thyssus, and the Church of St. Theodorus,‡ standing outside the city in the place which is called Rhesias, and the Church of the Martyr Thecla, which is near the harbour named after Julian, and that of St. Theodota in the suburb which is called Hebdomon. All these were built from their foundations by this Emperor during the reign of his uncle Justin, and are not easy to describe in words, while it is impossible to admire them sufficiently when beholding them. My narrative is now attracted to the Church of St. Agathonicus,§ and I am forced to mention it,

---

* 'S. Platonis ædes ab Anastasio Dicoro primum ædificata est, qui in eam decem columnas sculptas ex Thessalonica intulit, quarum duæ in Chalceno a Lacapeno postea translatæ sunt. De novo instauratam a Justiniano. At cum postmodum illius tectum laboraret, novum confecit, murosque quibus incumbebat, firmiores reddidit Basilius Macedo.' —Ducange, lib. iv., p. 92.

† 'S. Mocii Martyris templum, a Constantino Magno ædificatum. Codinus ait non de novo ædificatam fuisse a Constantino sed cum fanum esset deorum, illud expurgasse, dejectes simulacris ac idolis.'— Ducange, lib. iv., p. 89.

‡ This church is on the same plan as that of Myra.—V. Fergusson, p. 966. (L.)

§ 'S. Agathonici templum forma dromica ædificatum a Constantino Magno. Deinde in Angustiorem formam excitatum a Justiniano.

though I have no longer voice nor words befitting such a work: let it be sufficient for me to have said thus much of it; I will leave the description of its beauty and sumptuousness in all respects to others to whom the subject is fresh, and who are not wearied out by their labours.

V. Finding other churches in what is called the Anaplus, and along the coast of the opposite continent, which were not worthy to be dedicated to any of the saints, as also round the gulf which the natives call Ceras,* after the name of Ceroessa, the mother of Byzans, who was the founder of the city, he showed a royal munificence in all of them, as I will presently prove, having first said a few words about the glory which the sea adds to Byzantium.

The prosperity of Byzantium is increased by the sea which enfolds it, contracting itself into straits, and connecting itself with the ocean, thus rendering the city remarkably beautiful, and affording a safe protection in its harbours to seafarers, so as to cause it to be well supplied with provisions and abounding with all necessaries; for the two seas which are on either side of it, that is to say the Ægean and that which is called the Euxine, which meet at the east part of the city and dash together as they mingle their waves, separate the continent by their currents, and add to the beauty of the city while they surround it. It is, therefore, encompassed by three straits connected with one another, arranged so as to minister both to its elegance and its convenience, all of them most charming for sailing on, lovely to look at, and exceedingly safe for anchorage. The middle one of them,

---

Patriarches sedisse, coronatosque Imperatores quatuor, tandemque in Magno Palatio, cui adjacebat, inclusum sub Tiberio Mauricii socero.'
—Ducange, lib. iv., p. 81. (L.)

* Κέρας = horn. (S.)

which leads from the Euxine Sea, makes straight for the city as though to adorn it. Upon either side of it lie the several continents, between whose shores it is confined, and seems to foam proudly with its waves because it passes over both Asia and Europe in order to reach the city; you would think that you beheld a river flowing towards you with a gentle current. That which is on the left hand of it rests on either side upon widely extended shores, and displays the groves, the lovely meadows, and all the other charms of the opposite continent in full view of the city. As it makes its way onward towards the south, receding as far as possible from Asia, it becomes wider; but even then its waves continue to encircle the city as far as the setting of the sun. The third arm of the sea joins the first one upon the right hand, starting from the place called Sycae,* and washes the greater part of the northern shore of the city, ending in a bay. Thus the sea encircles the city like a crown, the interval consisting of the land lying between it in sufficient quantity to form a clasp for the crown of waters. This gulf is always calm, and never crested into waves, as though a barrier were placed there to the billows, and all storms were shut out from thence, through reverence for the city. Whenever strong winds and gales fall upon these seas and this strait, ships, when they once reach the entrance of this gulf, run the rest of their voyage unguided, and make the shore at random; for the gulf extends for a distance of more than forty stadia in circumference, and the whole of it is a harbour, so that when a ship is moored there the stern rests on the sea and the bows on the land, as though the two elements contended with one another to see which of them could be of the greatest service to the city.

VI. Such is the appearance of this gulf; but the Emperor

* Συκαί = fig-trees. (S.)

Justinian rendered it more lovely by the beauty of the buildings with which he surrounded it; for on the left side of it, he, to speak briefly, altered the Church of St. Laurentius the Martyr, which formerly was without windows and very dark,* into the appearance which it now presents; and in front of it he built the Church of the Virgin, in the place which is called Blachernæ, as I described a little above. Behind it he built a new church to SS. Priscus and Nicolaus, renewing the whole building. This is an especially favourite resort of the people of Byzantium, partly from their respect and reverence for the saints, which were their countrymen, and partly to enjoy the beauty of the situation of the church; for the Emperor drove back the waves of the sea, and laid the foundations as far among the billows as possible. At the upper part of the gulf, in a very steep and precipitous place, there was an ancient Church of SS. Cosmas and Damianus; where once these saints appeared on a sudden to the Emperor as he lay grievously sick and apparently at the point of death, given up by his physicians, and already reckoned as dead, and miraculously made him whole. In order to repay their goodness, as far as a mortal man may do, he entirely altered and renewed the former building, which was unseemly and humble, and not worthy to be dedicated to such great saints, adorned the new church with beauty and size and brilliant light, and gave it many other things which it did not formerly possess. When men are suffering from diseases beyond the reach of physicians, and despair of human aid, they resort to the only hope which is left to them, and sail through this gulf in boats to this church. As soon as they begin their voyage they see this church

---

* The very ancient church at Ratisbon, known as the 'Alter Dom,' or 'Stephan's Kirchlein,' is believed to have been originally built without windows. (S.)

standing as though on a lofty citadel, made beautiful by the gratitude of the Emperor, and affording them hope that they too may partake of the benefits which flow from thence.

On the opposite side of the gulf the Emperor built a church which did not exist before, quite close to the shore of the gulf, and dedicated it to the Martyr Anthimus. The base of this temple, laved by the gentle wash of the sea, is most picturesque; for no lofty billows dash against its stones, nor does the wave resound like that of the open sea, or burst into masses of foam, but gently glides up to the land, silently laps against it, and quietly retreats. Beyond this is a level and very smooth court, adorned all round with marble columns, and rendered beautiful by its view of the sea. Next to this is a portico, beyond which rises the church, of a quadrangular form, adorned with beautiful marble and gildings. Its length only exceeds its breadth far enough to give room for the sanctuary, in which the sacred mysteries are performed, on the side which is turned towards the rising sun; such is the description of it.

VII. Beyond this, at the very mouth of the gulf, stands the Church of the Martyr Irene,* which the Emperor has so magnificently constructed that I could not competently describe it; for, contending with the sea in his desire to beautify the gulf, he has built these churches as though he were placing gems upon a necklace; however, since I have mentioned this Church of Irene, it will not be foreign to my purpose to describe what took place there. Here, from ancient times, rested the remains of no fewer

---

* 'St. Irene Martyris templum, ultra ædem S. Anthimi, ad ipsum Sinus Ostium ædificavit Justinianus. Verum S. Irenes ædis Sycænæ, seu Sycis proximæ, non fuit conditor Justinianus sed instaurator.'— Ducange, lib. iv., p. 103. (L.)

than forty saints, who were Roman soldiers, and were enrolled in the twelfth legion, which formerly was stationed in the city of Melitene, in Armenia; now, when the masons dug in the place which I just spoke of, they found a chest with an inscription stating that it contained the remains of these men. This chest, which had been forgotten, was at that time purposely brought to light by God, both with the object of proving to all men with how great joy He received the gifts of the Emperor, and also in order to reward his good works by the bestowal of a still greater favour; for the Emperor Justinian was in ill-health, and a large collection of humours in his knee caused him great pain. His illness arose from his own fault; for during all the days which precede the Paschal Feast, and are called fast-days, he practised a severe abstinence, unfit not only for a prince, but even for a man who took no part in political matters. He used to pass two days entirely without food, and that, too, although he rose from his bed at early dawn to watch over the State, whose business he ever transacted, both by actions and words, early in the morning, at midday, and at night with equal zeal; for though he would retire to rest late at night, he would almost immediately arise, as though disliking his bed. Whenever he did take nourishment, he refrained from wine, bread, and all other food, eating only herbs, and those wild ones which had been for a long time pickled in salt and vinegar, whilst water was his only drink. Yet he never ate to repletion even of these; but whenever he dined, he would merely taste this food, and then push it away, never eating sufficient. From this regimen his disease gathered strength, defying the efforts of physicians, and for a long time the Emperor suffered from these pains. During this time, hearing of the discovery of the relics, he disregarded human art, and commended himself to them, deriving health from his faith in them, and finding healing in his bitterest need from his true faith; for as soon as the priests placed the paten upon his knee, the disease at once vanished—forced out of a body dedicated to God. Not wishing that this matter should be disputed, God displayed a great sign as a testimony to this miracle. Oil suddenly poured forth from the holy relics, overflowed the chest, and besprinkled the feet and the purple garment of the Emperor. Wherefore his tunic, thus saturated, is preserved in the palace as a testimony of what then took place, and for the healing of those who in future time may suffer from incurable disorders.

VIII. Thus did the Emperor Justinian adorn the gulf which is called the Horn; he also added great beauty to the shores of the other two straits, of which I lately made mention, in the following manner. There were two churches dedicated to St. Michael the Archangel, opposite to one another, on either side of the strait, the one in the place called Anaplus* on the left hand as one sails into the Euxine Sea, and the other on the opposite shore. This place was called Pröochthus by the ancients—I suppose because it projects a long way from that shore—and is now called Brochi, the ignorance of the inhabitants having in process of time corrupted the name. The priests of these two churches, perceiving that they were dilapidated by age, and fearing that they might presently fall down upon them, besought the Emperor to restore them both to their former condition; for in his reign it was not possible for a church either to be built, or to be restored when ruined, except from the royal treasury, and that not only in Byzantium, but also everywhere throughout the Roman Empire. The Emperor, as soon as he

* Near the village of Kourou, Cheshmeh.—'Murray's 'Guide to Turkey and Asia Minor,' etc., 1878, p. 106. (L.)

obtained this opportunity, demolished both of them to the foundation, that no part of their former unseemliness might be left. He rebuilt the one in Anaplus* in the following manner. He formed the shore into a curve within a mole of stone, which he erected as a protection to the harbour, and changed the sea-beach into the appearance of a market; for the sea, which is there very smooth, exchanges its produce with the land, and seafaring merchants, mooring their barques alongside the mole, exchange the merchandise from their decks for the produce of the country. Beyond this sea-side market stands forth the vestibule of the church, whose marble vies in colour with ripe fruit and snow. Those who take their walks in this quarter are charmed with the beauty of the stone, are delighted with the view of the sea, and are refreshed with the breezes from the water and the hills which rise upon the land. A circular portico surrounds the church on all sides except the east. In the midst of it stands the church, adorned with marble of various colours. Above it is suspended a domed roof. Who, after viewing it, could speak worthily of the lofty porticoes, of the buildings within, of the grace of the marble with which the walls and foundations are everywhere encrusted? In addition to all this, a great quantity of gold is everywhere spread over the church, as though it grew upon it. In describing this, I have also described the Church of St. John the Baptist,† which the Emperor

---

* 'S. Michaelis templum in Anaplo ædificavit Constantinus Magnus. Cum vero Anaplus proprie dicatur littus Bospori Europæanum, ut alibi indicatum, locum distinctius designat Cedrenus, ἐν τῷ ᾿Αναπλῳ καὶ Σωσθενίῳ. Ædem S. Michaelis Sosthenianam de novo et a fundamentis instauravit Justinianus Magnus ut et alteram quam in opposito littore Asiatico ab eodem Constantino Magno ædificatam narrat Nicephorus.'
—Ducange, lib. iv., pp. 130, 131. (L.)

† 'Joannis Baptistæ in Hebdomo templum excitavit Theodosius

Justinian lately erected in his honour in the place called Hebdomon; for both the two churches are very like each other, except only that the Church of the Baptist does not happen to stand by the sea-shore.

The Church of the Archangel, in the place called Anaplus, is built in the above manner; now upon the opposite shore there is a place at a little distance from the sea, which is level, and raised high upon a mass of stones. Here has been built a church in honour of the Archangel, of exceeding beauty, of the largest size, and in costliness worthy of being dedicated to the Archangel Michael by the Emperor Justinian. Not far from this church, he restored a church of the Virgin, which had fallen into ruins long before, whose magnificence it would take long to examine and to express in words; but here a long-expected part of our history finds its place.

IX. Upon this shore there stood from ancient times a beautiful palace: the whole of this the Emperor Justinian dedicated to God, exchanging present enjoyment for the reward of his piety hereafter, in the following manner. There were at Byzantium a number of women who were prostituted in a brothel, not willingly, but compelled to exercise their profession; for under pressure of poverty they were compelled by the procurer who kept them to

---

Magnus et in eo nuper inventum, et in urbem allatum caput sancti Præcursoris reposuit rotundo tecto Theodosius Magnus condidit. A Justiniano excitatam, seu potius instauratam prodit Procopius. Denique hanc rursum instauravit Basilius Macedo. Ea in latere ad solis ortum pertinente sita est, a Turcis maxima ex parte diruta, ubi aliquot columnæ marmoreæ extremam rapinam metuentes supersunt, sed paucæ ex multis ablatis. Quam, autem illa sumptuosa fuisset cum alia vestigia indicant, tum cisterna Boni paulò supra eam sita, longa 300 passus, columnis et concameratione spoliata, in qua nunc horti virent.'
—Ducange, lib. iv., pp. 68, 69. Cisternam Boni. Cameris cylindricis tectam, extruxit Bonus Patricius et Magister cui Heraclius Imp., contra Persas profecturus, urbis custodiam commisit.'—Ducange, lib. i., p. 80. (L.)

act in this manner, and to offer themselves to unknown and casual passers-by. There was here from ancient times a guild of brothel-keepers, who not only carried on their profession in this building, but publicly bought their victims in the market, and forced them into an unchaste life. However, the Emperor Justinian and the Empress Theodora, who performed all their works of piety in common, devised the following scheme. They cleansed the State from the pollution of these brothels, drove out the procurers, and set free these women who had been driven to evil courses by their poverty, providing them with a sufficient maintenance, and enabling them to live chaste as well as free. This was arranged in the following manner: they changed the palace, which stood on the right hand as one sails into the Euxine Sea, into a magnificent convent, to serve as a refuge for women who had repented of their former life, in order that there spending their lives in devotion to God, and in continual works of piety, they might wash away the sins of their former life of shame; wherefore this dwelling of these women is called from their work by the name of the Penitentiary. The princes endowed this convent with large revenues, and furnished it with many buildings of exceeding great beauty and costliness for the comfort of these women, so that none of them might be forced by any circumstances to relax their practice of chastity. So much then for this part of the subject.

As one sails from this place towards the Euxine Sea, there is a lofty promontory jutting out from the shore of the strait, upon which stood a Church of the Martyr St. Pan-telëemon,* which, having been originally carelessly built, and having been much ruined by lapse of time, was taken

---

* 'Some ruins of this still remain near Fort Yousha, on the Asiatic shore of the Bosphorus.'—Murray's 'Guide,' p. 118. (L.)

down by the Emperor Justinian, who built the church which now stands there with the greatest magnificence, and both preserved the honour due to the martyr and added beauty to the strait by building on each side of it the churches which I have mentioned. Beyond this church, in a place which is called Argyronium, there was, in old times, a hospital for poor men afflicted with incurable diseases, which having in the course of time fallen into the last stage of decay, he most zealously restored, to serve as a refuge for those who were thus afflicted. Near this place there is a district by the sea-side called Mochadius, which is also called Hieron. Here he built a temple in honour of the Archangel of remarkable splendour, and in no respect inferior to those Churches of the Archangel, of which I spoke just now. He also built a church dedicated to St. Tryphon the Martyr, decorated with much labour and time to an indescribable pitch of beauty, in that street of the city which is called by the name of 'The Stork.' Furthermore, he built a church in the Hebdomon, in honour of the martyrs Menas[*] and Menæus; and finding that the Church of St. Ias the Martyr, which is on the left hand as one enters the Golden Gate, was in ruins, he restored it with a lavish expenditure. This is what was done by the Emperor Justinian in connection with the churches in Byzantium; but to describe all his works throughout the entire Roman Empire in detail, is a difficult task, and altogether impossible to express in words, but, whenever I shall have to make mention of the name of any city or district, I shall take the opportunity of describing the churches in it.

X. The above were the works of the Emperor Justinian

---

[*] 'SS. Menæ et Menæi Martyrum ædem excitavit in Hebdomo Justinianus.'—Ducange, lib. iv., p. 88. (S.)

upon the churches of Constantinople and its suburbs; but as to the other buildings constructed by him, it would not be easy to mention them all. However, to sum up matters, he rebuilt and much improved in beauty the largest and most considerable part both of the city and of the palace, which had been burned down and levelled with the ground. It appears unnecessary for me to enter into particulars on this subject at present, since it has all been minutely described in my 'History of the Wars.' For the present I shall only say this much, that the vestibule of the palace and that which is called Chalce, as far as what is known as the House of Ares, and outside the palace the public baths of Zeuxippus,* and the great porticoes and all the buildings on either hand, as far as the forum of Constantine, are the works of this Emperor. In addition to these, he restored and added great magnificence to the house named after Hormisdas, which stands close to the palace, rendering it worthy of the palace, to which he joined it, and thereby rendered it much more roomy and worthy of admiration on that side.

In front of the palace there is a forum surrounded with columns. The Byzantines call this forum the Augustæum. I mentioned it in a former part of this work, when, after describing the Church of St. Sophia, I spoke of the brazen statue of the Emperor, which stands upon a very lofty column of stones as a memorial of that work. On the eastern side of this forum stands the Senate House, which baffles description by its costliness and entire arrangement, and which was the work of the Emperor Justinian. Here at the beginning of every year the Roman Senate holds an annual festival, according to the custom of the State.

---

* 'The finest marbles were taken from the Baths of Zeuxippus, and used by Mahomet II. for building his Mosque, etc.'—V. Texier and Pullan, p. 161. (L.)

Six columns stand in front of it, two of them having between them that wall of the Senate House which looks towards the west, while the four others stand a little beyond it. These columns are all white in colour, and in size, I imagine, are the largest columns in the whole world. They form a portico covered by a circular dome-shaped roof. The upper parts of this portico are all adorned with marble equal in beauty to that of the columns, and are wonderfully ornamented with a number of statues standing on the roof.

Not far from this forum stands the Emperor's palace, which, as I have said before, was almost entirely rebuilt by the Emperor Justinian. To describe it all in words is impossible, but it will suffice for future generations to know that it was all the work of this Emperor. As, according to the proverb, we know the lion by his claw, so my readers will learn the magnificence of this palace from the entrance-hall. This entrance-hall is the building called Chalce; its four walls stand in a quadrangular form, and are very lofty; they are equal to one another in all respects, except that those on the north and south sides are a little shorter than the others. In each angle of them stands a pier of very well-wrought stone, reaching from the floor to the summit of the wall, quadrangular in form and joining the wall on one of its sides: they do not in any way destroy the beauty of the place, but even add ornament to it by the symmetry of their position. Above them are suspended eight arches, four of which support the roof, which rises above the whole work in a spherical form, whilst the others, two of which rest on the neighbouring wall towards the south and two towards the north, support the arched roof which is suspended over those spaces. The entire ceiling is decorated with paintings, not formed of melted wax poured upon it,

3—2

but composed of tiny stones adorned with all manner of colours, imitating human figures and everything else in nature. I will now describe the subjects of these paintings. Upon either side are wars and battles, and the capture of numberless cities, some in Italy, and some in Libya. Here the Emperor Justinian conquers by his General Belisarius; and here the General returns to the Emperor, bringing with him his entire army unscathed, and offers to him the spoils of victory, kings, and kingdoms, and all that is most valued among men. In the midst stand the Emperor and the Empress Theodora, both of them seeming to rejoice and hold high festival in honour of their victory over the kings of the Vandals and the Goths, who approach them as prisoners of war led in triumph. Around them stands the Senate of Rome, all in festal array, which is shown in the mosaic by the joy which appears on their countenances; they swell with pride and smile upon the Emperor, offering him honours as though to a demi-god, after his magnificent achievements. The whole interior, not only the upright parts, but also the floor itself, is encrusted with beautiful marbles, reaching up to the mosaics of the ceiling. Of these marbles, some are of a Spartan stone equal to emerald, while some resemble a flame of fire; the greater part of them are white, yet not a plain white, but ornamented with wavy lines of dark blue.* So much for this building.

XI. As one sails from the Propontis towards the eastern part of the city, there is a public bath on the left hand which is called the Baths of Arcadius, and which forms an

---

* 'The dome of a spacious quadrangle was supported on massy pillars; the pavement and walls encrusted with many coloured marbles—the emerald green of Laconia, the fiery red, and the white Phrygian stone, intersected with veins of a sea-green hue: the Mosaic paintings of the dome and sides represented the glories of the African and Italian triumphs.'—Gibbon, ch. xl. (S.)

ornament to the city of Constantinople, great as it is. Here our Emperor constructed a court standing outside the city, intended as a promenade for the inhabitants, and a mooring-place for those who sail past it. This court is lighted by the sun when rising, but is conveniently shaded when he proceeds towards the west. Round it the sea flows quietly with a gentle stream, coming like a river from the main sea, so that those who are taking their walks in it are able to converse with those who are sailing; for the sea reaches up to the basement of the court with great depth, navigable for ships, and by its remarkable calm enables those on the water and on the land to converse with one another. Such is the side of the court which looks upon the sea, adorned with the view over it, and refreshed with the gentle breezes from it. Its basement, its columns, and its entablature are all covered with marble of great beauty, whose colour is of a most brilliant white, which glitters magnificently in the rays of the sun; moreover, many statues adorn it, some of brass and some of marble, composing a sight well worth mention; one would conjecture that they were the work of Phidias the Athenian, of Lysippus of Sicyon, or of Praxiteles. Here also is a statue of the Empress Theodora on a column, which was erected in her honour by the city as an offering of gratitude for this court. The face of the statue is beautiful, but falls short of the beauty of the Empress, since it is utterly impossible for any mere human workmen to express her loveliness, or to imitate it in a statue; the column is of porphyry, and clearly shows by its magnificent appearance that it carries the Empress, before one sees the statue.

I will now explain the Emperor's works to afford an abundant supply of water to the city. In summer-time the imperial city used for the most part to suffer from scarcity of water, although at other seasons it had sufficient ; for at that time, in consequence of the drought, the fountains flowed less plenteously than at other seasons, and supplied the aqueducts of the city very sparingly. Wherefore the Emperor devised the following plan. In the Portico of the Emperor, where the advocates, and magistrates, and other persons connected with the law transact business, there is a very lofty court of great length and width, quadrangular in shape, and surrounded with columns, which is not constructed upon an earthen foundation, but upon the rock itself. Four porticos surround this court, one upon each side of it. The Emperor Justinian excavated one of these porticos, that upon the south side, to a great depth, and stored up there the superfluity of water from the other seasons for use in summer. These cisterns receive the overflow from the aqueducts, when they are too full of water, giving them a place to overflow into, and afford a supply in time of need when water becomes scarce. Thus did the Emperor Justinian arrange that the people of Byzantium should not want for sweet water.

He also built new palaces elsewhere, one in the Heræum,* which is now called the Hiereum, and in the place called Jucundiana. I am unable to describe either the magnificence or exquisite workmanship, or the size of these palaces in a manner worthy of the subject. Suffice it to say that these palaces stand there, and were built in the presence and according to the plans of Justinian, who disregarded nothing except expense, which was so large that the mind is unable to grasp it. Here also he con-

---

* ' On the Asiatic shore of the Propontis, at a small distance to the east of Chalcedon, the costly palace and gardens of Heræum were prepared for the summer residence of Justinian, and more especially of Theodora.'—Gibbon, ch. xl. (S.)

structed a sheltered harbour, which did not exist before. Finding that the shore was exposed on both sides to the winds and the violence of the waves, he arranged a place of refuge for mariners in the following manner: he constructed what are called chests, of countless number and of great size, flung them into the sea on each side of the beach in an oblique direction, and by continually placing fresh layers in order upon the others, formed two walls in the sea opposite to one another, reaching from the depths below to the surface of the water on which the ships sail; upon this he flung rough stones, which when struck by the waves break their force, so that when a strong wind blows in the winter season, everything between these walls remains calm, an interval being left between them to serve as an entrance for ships into the harbour. Here also he built the churches which I formerly mentioned, and also porticos, market-places, public baths, and everything else of that sort; so that this palace in no respect falls short of that within the city. He also built another harbour on the opposite continent, in the place which is called after the name of Eutropius, not very far from the Heræum, constructed in the same manner as that which I mentioned above.

The above are, described as briefly as possible, the works of the Emperor Justinian in the imperial city. I will now describe the only thing which remains. Since the Emperor dwells here, a multitude of men of all nations comes into the city from all the world, in consequence of the vast extent of the empire, each one of them led thither either by business, by hope, or by chance, many of whom, whose affairs at home have fallen into disorder, come with the intention of offering some petition to the Emperor. These persons, forced to dwell in the city on account of some present or threatened misfortune, in addition to their other trouble are also in want of lodging, being unable to pay for a dwelling-place during their stay in the city. This source of misery was removed from them by the Emperor Justinian and the Empress Theodora, who built very large hospices as places of refuge in time of need for such unfortunate persons as these, close to the sea, in the place which is called the Stadium, I suppose because in former times it was used for public games.

NOTE.—For the interesting church of the Chora, see Appendix.

BOOK II.

I. The new churches which the Emperor Justinian built in Constantinople and its suburbs, the churches which were ruinous through age, and which he restored, and all the other buildings which he erected there, are described in my previous book; it remains that we should proceed to the fortresses with which he encircled the frontier of the Roman territory. This subject requires great labour, and indeed is almost impossible to describe; we are not about to describe the Pyramids, that celebrated work of the Kings of Egypt, in which labour was wasted on a useless freak, but all the strong places by means of which our Emperor preserved the empire, and so fortified it as to render vain any attempt of the barbarians against the Romans. I think I should do well to start from the Median frontier.

When the Medes retired from the country of the Romans, restoring to them the city of Amida,* as has been narrated in my 'History of the Wars,' the Emperor Anastasius took great pains to build a wall round an, at that time, unimportant village named Dara, which he observed was situated near the Persian frontier, and to form it into a

* Now Diarbekr, on the Tigris, about twelve miles from Nisebin.

city which would act as a bulwark against the enemy. Since, however, by the terms of the treaty formerly made by the Emperor Theodosius with the Persians, it was forbidden that either party should build any new fortress on their own ground in the neighbourhood of the frontier, the Persians urged that this was forbidden by the articles of the peace, and hindered the work with all their power, although their attention was diverted from it by their war with the Huns. The Romans, perceiving that on account of this war they were unprepared, pushed on their building all the more vigorously, being eager to finish the work before the enemy should bring their war against the Huns to a close and march against themselves. Being alarmed through their suspicions of the enemy, and constantly expecting an attack, they did not construct their building carefully, but the quickness of building into which they were forced by their excessive hurry prevented their work being secure; for speed and safety are never wont to go together, nor is swiftness often accompanied by accuracy. They therefore built the city-walls in this hurried fashion, not making a wall which would defy the enemy, but raising it barely to the necessary height; nor did they even place the stones in their right positions or arrange them in due order, or fill the interstices with mortar. In a short time, therefore, since the towers, through their insecure construction, were far from being able to withstand snow and hot sun, most of them fell into ruins. Thus was the first wall built round the city of Dara.*

* 'Military architecture had a special character during the reign of Justinian, and his successors departed but little from the principles laid down by the engineers of his time. The walls were flanked with towers, usually round. The most commanding part was occupied by a square redoubt defended at the angles by towers. The gates were protected by an advanced work. The fortifications of many towns in Mesopotamia, *e.g.* Edessa, date from the time of Justinian, and are constructed on the same principle.'—Abridged from Texier and Pullan, pp. 23, 24. (L.)

It occurred to the Emperor Justinian that the Persians would not, as far as lay in their power, permit this Roman fortress to stand threatening them, but that they would march against it with their entire force, and use every

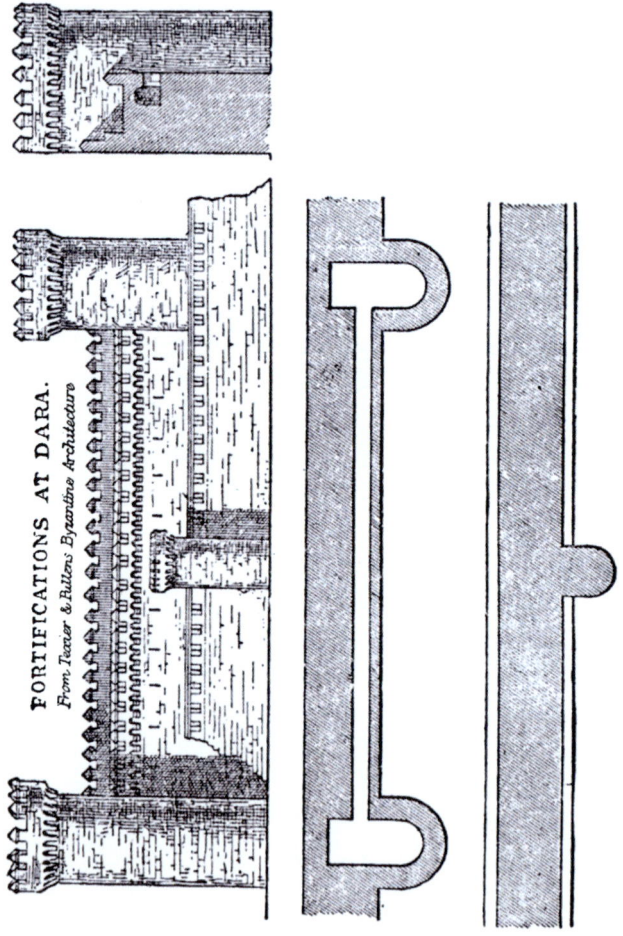

FORTIFICATIONS AT DARA.
From Texier & Pullens Byzantine Architecture

device to assault its walls on equal terms; and that a number of elephants would accompany them, bearing wooden towers upon their backs, which towers instead of foundations would rest upon the elephants, who—and this was the worst of all—could manœuvre round the city at the pleasure of the enemy, and carry a wall which could be moved whithersoever its masters might think fit; and the enemy, mounted upon these towers, would shoot down upon the heads of the Romans within the walls, and assail them from above; they would also pile up mounds of earth against the walls, and bring up to them all the machines used in sieges; while if any misfortune should befall the city of Dara, which was an outwork of the entire Roman Empire and a standing menace to the enemy's country, the evil would not rest there, but the whole state would be endangered to a great extent. Moved by these considerations he determined to fortify the place in a manner worthy of its value.

In the first place,* therefore, since the wall was, as I have described, very low, and therefore easily assailable, he rendered it inaccessible and altogether impregnable. He placed stones which so contracted the original battlements as only to leave small traces of them, like windows, allowing just so much opening to them as a hand could be passed through, so that passages were left through which arrows could be shot against the assailants. Above these he built a wall to a height of about thirty feet, not making the wall of the same thickness all the way to the top, lest the foundations should be over-weighted by the mass above, and the whole work be ruined; but he surrounded the upper part with a course of stones, and built a portico extending round the entire circuit of the walls,

* 'The fortifications of Dara were almost entirely rebuilt by the Emperor Anastasius, A.D. 503. Hastily constructed, they fell into ruins in a few years. Justinian rebuilt the town, A.D. 537. The line of its ramparts, which were built of large blocks of limestone, can be traced throughout, certain portions being still 30 feet high.'—Abridged from Texier and Pullan, p. 53. (L.)

above which he placed the battlements, so that the wall was throughout constructed of two stories, and the towers of three stories, which could be manned by the defenders to repel the attacks of the enemy; for over the middle of the towers he constructed a vaulted roof, and again built new battlements above it, thus making them into a fortification consisting of three stories.

After this, though he saw, as I have said before, that many of the towers had after a short time fallen into ruin, yet he was not able to take them down, because the enemy were always close at hand, watching their opportunity, and always trying to find some unprotected part of the fortifications. He therefore devised the following plan: he left these towers where they were, and outside of each of them he constructed another building with great skill, in a quadrangular form, well and securely built. In the same manner he securely protected the ruinous parts of the walls with a second wall. One of these towers, which was called the Watch-tower, he seized an opportunity of demolishing, rebuilt it securely, and everywhere removed all fear of want of strength from the walls. He wisely built the outside part of the wall to a sufficient height, in due proportion; outside of it he dug a ditch, not in the way in which men usually make one, but in a small space, and in a different fashion. With what object he did this, I will now explain.

The greater part of the walls are inaccessible to besiegers, because they do not stand upon level ground, nor in such a manner as would favour an attack, but upon high precipitous rocks where it would not be possible to undermine them, or to make any assault upon them; but upon the side turned towards the south, the ground, which is soft and earthy and easily dug, renders the city assailable. Here, therefore, he dug a crescent-shaped ditch, deep and wide, and reaching to a considerable distance. Each end of this ditch joined the city wall, and by filling it with water he rendered it altogether impassable to the enemy. On the inner side of it he built a second wall, upon which during a siege the Roman soldiers keep guard, without fear for the walls themselves and for the other outwork which stands before the city. Between the city wall and this outwork, opposite the gate which leads towards Ammodius, there was a great mound, from which the enemy were able to drive mines towards the city unperceived. This he entirely removed, and levelled the spot, so as to put it out of the enemy's power to assault the place from thence.

II. Thus did Justinian fortify this stronghold;* he also constructed reservoirs of water between the city walls and the outwork, and very close to the Church of St. Bartholomew the Apostle, on the west side. A river runs from the suburb called Corde, distant about two miles from the city. Upon either side of it rise two exceedingly rugged

---

* 'The fortifications of Dara,' says Gibbon, 'may represent the military architecture of the age. The city was surrounded by two walls, and the interval between them, of fifty paces, afforded a retreat to the cattle of the besieged. The inner wall was a monument of strength and beauty : it measured sixty feet from the ground, and the height of the towers was one hundred feet ; the loopholes, from whence an enemy might be annoyed with missile weapons, were small, but numerous ; the soldiers were placed along the rampart, under the shelter of double galleries, and a third platform, spacious and secure, was raised on the summit of the towers. The exterior wall seems to have been less lofty, but more solid ; and each tower was protected by a quadrangular bulwark. A hard rocky soil resisted the tools of the miners, and on the south-east, where the ground was more tractable, their approach was retarded by a new work, which advanced in the shape of a half-moon. The double and treble ditches were filled with a stream of water ; and in the management of the river, the most skilful labour was employed to supply the inhabitants, to distress the besiegers, and to prevent the mischiefs of a natural or artificial inundation.'—Gibbon, ch. xl. (S.) See Note, page 58.

mountains. Between the slopes of these mountains the river runs as far as the city, and since it flows at the foot of them, it is not possible for an enemy to divert or meddle with its stream, for they cannot force it out of the hollow ground. It is directed into the city in the following manner. The inhabitants have built a great channel leading to the walls, the mouth of which is closed with numerous thick bars of iron, some upright and some placed crosswise, so as to enable the water to enter the city, without injury to the strength of its fortifications. Thus the river enters the city, and after having filled these reservoirs, and been led hither and thither at the pleasure of the inhabitants, passes into another part of the city, where there is an outfall constructed for it in the same way as its entrance. The river in its progress through the flat country made the city in former times easy to be besieged, for it was not difficult for an enemy to encamp there, because water was plentiful. The Emperor Justinian considered this state of things, and tried to find some remedy for it; God, however, assisted him in his difficulty, took the matter into His own hands, and without delay ensured the safety of the city. This took place in the following manner.

One of the garrison of the city, either in consequence of a dream or led of his own accord to it, collected together a great number of the workmen engaged in building the fortifications, and ordered them to dig a long trench in a certain place, which he pointed out to them, a considerable distance within the city wall, declaring that they would there find sweet water flowing out of the ground. He dug this trench in a circular form, making the depth of it for the most part about fifteen feet. This work proved the saving of the city, not through any foresight of the workmen, yet, by means of this trench, what would have been a misfortune was turned into a great advantage to the Romans; for, as during this time very heavy rain fell, the river, of which I just spoke, raged outside the fortifications and rose to a great height, being unable to proceed, because when it was swollen to such a size neither the channel nor the entrances in the wall were large enough to contain it, as they had been before. It consequently piled up its waters against the wall, rising to a great height and depth, and in some places was stagnant, and in others rough and violent. It at once overthrew the outwork, swept away a great part of the city wall, forced its way through the city gates, and, running with a great body of water, occupied almost the whole city, invading both the market-place, the narrower streets, and the houses themselves, swept off from them a great mass of furniture, wooden vessels, and such like things, and then, falling into this trench, disappeared under ground. Not many days afterwards it reappeared near to the city of Theodosiopolis, at a place about forty miles distant from the city of Dara, where it was recognised by the things which it had swept away out of the houses at Dara, for there the whole mass of them reappeared. Since that period, in time of peace and quiet, the river flows through the midst of the city, fills the reservoirs with water, and passes out of the city through the outfall especially constructed for it by the builders of the city, which I described above, and, as it supplies that region with water, becomes a great boon to the inhabitants of the neighbourhood. When, however, a hostile army advances to besiege the city, they close the passages through the iron gratings with what are called sluice-doors, and at once force the river to change its course and to flow into the trench and the subterranean gulf beyond, so that the enemy suffer from want of water and are at once obliged to raise the siege.

Indeed Mirrhanes, the Persian general, in the reign of Cabades, came thither to besiege the city, and was compelled by all these difficulties to retire baffled after a short time; and a long while afterwards, Chosroes himself advanced with the same intentions, and attacked the city with a numerous army; but being driven to great straits through want of water, and perceiving the height of the walls, he imagined the place to be entirely impregnable, gave up his project, and straightway retired into Persia, being out-generalled by the foresight of the Roman Emperor.

III. Such were the works of the Emperor Justinian in the city of Dara. I shall now describe what he arranged to prevent any second misfortune happening to the city from the river, in which matter his wishes were manifestly assisted by Heaven. There was one Chryses of Alexandria, a clever engineer, who served the Emperor as an architect, and constructed most of the works both in the city of Dara and in the rest of the country. This Chryses was absent when the misfortune from the river befell the city of Dara; when he heard of it, he retired to bed in great grief, and dreamed the following dream: A figure of more than human stature appeared to him, and showed and explained to him a device which would protect the city from any dangerous inundation of the river. He, conceiving this idea to be divinely inspired, at once wrote an account of the device and of the vision, and sent it to the Emperor, giving a sketch of what he had been taught in his dream. It happened that not long before this a message reached the Emperor from the city of Dara, giving him an account of what had happened with the river. Thereupon the Emperor, disturbed and alarmed at what had taken place, straightway summoned those most celebrated architects, Anthemius and Isidorus, whom I have mentioned before. He informed them of what had happened, and inquired what arrangement could be devised to prevent this mischief befalling the city a second time. Each of them described what he considered to be a suitable plan for this purpose; but the Emperor, evidently acting under a divine impulse, although he had not yet seen the letter of Chryses, miraculously invented and sketched out of his own mind the plan suggested by the dream. The interview terminated without the adoption of any distinct plan, and without their deciding upon what was to be done; but three days afterwards came a messenger to the Emperor, who brought the letter from Chryses, and who explained the form of the arrangement which he had seen in his dream. The Emperor now again sent for the architects, and ordered them to recall to mind their former ideas of what ought to be done. They repeated everything in order, both their own devices and the spontaneous inventions of the Emperor; after which the Emperor brought forward the messenger sent from Chryses, and showing them the letter and the sketch of what he had seen in his dream, caused them to wonder greatly, when they perceived how Heaven had assisted our Emperor in everything for the advantage of the Empire. The plan of the Emperor accordingly won the day, and triumphed over the art and learning of the architects. Chryses returned to the city of Dara, with orders from the Emperor to carry out the work which he had described with all speed, according to the plan revealed in the dream. He carried out his orders in the following manner.

In a place about forty feet distant from the outwork of the city, across the valley in which the river runs between the two mountains, he constructed a barrier of considerable height and width, joining each end of it to the mountain on either side, in such a manner that the water of the river in its strongest flood could never force its way through it.

This work is called by those who are learned in such matters a dam, or sluice, or whatever else they please. He did not build this barrier in a straight line, but in the form of a crescent, in order that its arch, which was turned against the stream of the water, might be better able to resist its violence. The upper and lower parts of this barrier are pierced with apertures, so that, when the river suddenly rises in flood, it is forced to stop there and to flow no further with the entire weight of its stream, but passing in small quantities through these apertures it gradually diminishes in violence and power, and the wall is never damaged by it; for the flow of water, collecting in the place which, as I have said before, is about forty feet in length, lying between the barrier and the outwork, is never unmanageable, but runs gently to its usual entrance, and thence is received in the artificial channel. As for the gate, which the fury of the river broke open in former times, he removed it from thence, and blocked up its site with enormous stones, because this gate, being situated on flat ground, was easily reached by the river when in flood; but he placed the gate not far off, in a lofty place in the most precipitous part of the circuit of the walls, which it was impossible for the river to reach. Thus did the Emperor arrange these matters.

The inhabitants of this city suffered greatly from the want of water, for there was no fountain springing out of the ground, nor was any water carried about the streets in an aqueduct, or stored up in cisterns; but those who lived in the streets through which the river passed could draw drinking-water from it without trouble, while those who dwelt at a distance from the course of the river had either to fetch their drinking-water with great trouble or to perish with thirst; however, the Emperor Justinian constructed a great aqueduct, by which he brought the water to every part of the city, and relieved the distress of the inhabitants. He also built two churches, that which is called the Great Church, and the Church of St. Bartholomew the Apostle.* Moreover, he built very spacious barracks for the soldiers, that they might not inconvenience the inhabitants.

Not long after this he restored the wall and outworks of the city of Amida, which had been built in former times, and were thought likely to fall into ruins; thus ensuring the safety of that city. I am now about to speak of his buildings in the forts which stand on the frontier of the territory of these cities.

IV. As one goes from the city of Dara towards the land of Persia, there lies on the left a tract entirely impassable for carriages or horses, extending to the distance of about two days' journey for a lightly-equipped traveller, ending in an abrupt and precipitous place called Rhabdium.† The land on each side of this road to Rhabdium belongs for a great distance to Persia. When I first saw this I was surprised at it, and inquired of the people of the country how it was that a road and tract belonging to the Romans should have enemy's land on each side of it. They answered, that this country once belonged to the Persians, but that at the request of the King of Persia one of the Roman Emperors gave a village abounding in vines near Martyropolis,‡ and received this region in exchange

* 'The Church of Dara is in a perfect state of preservation owing to the extreme solidity of its construction—a parallelogram 97·6 by 68·3. In the interior, the nave, with the adjoining chapels, forms a perfect square. A building adjoining, supposed to have been the baptistry, is ruined. Mr. Ainsworth says there are seven or eight churches in the town.'—Texier and Pullan, p. 52.

† ? Rabdiun, near Jezireh-ibn-Omar. A fine old castle. 'This appears to be the Rabdium of the Byzantines. The remains of an ancient bridge are seen crossing the Tigris at a short distance.'—Chesney's 'Euphrates.' (L.)

‡ Mejafarkîn, north-east of Diarbekr. (W.)

for it. The city of Rhabdium stands upon precipitous and wild rocks, which there rise to a wondrous height; below it is a region which they call 'the field of the Romans,' out of wonder, I suppose, at its belonging to the Romans, though it lies in the midst of the Persian country. This Roman field lies on flat ground, and is fruitful in all kinds of crops; one might conjecture this from the fact that the Persian frontier surrounds it on every side.

There is a very celebrated fort in Persia, named Sisauranum, which the Emperor Justinian once captured and razed to the ground; taking prisoners a great number of Persian cavalry, together with their leader Bleschanes. This place lies at a distance of two days' journey from Dara for a lightly-equipped traveller, and is about three miles distant from Rhabdium. It was formerly unguarded, and altogether neglected by the Romans, so that it never received from them any garrison, fortification, or any other benefit, wherefore the peasants who tilled this country, of which I just spoke, besides the ordinary taxes, paid an annual tribute of fifty gold pieces to the Persians, in order that they might possess their lands and enjoy the produce of them in security. All this was altered for them by the Emperor Justinian, who enclosed Rhabdium with fortifications, which he built upon the summit of the mountain which rises there, and, taking advantage of the position of the ground, rendered it impossible for the enemy to approach it. As those who dwelt in it were in want of water, there being no springs on the top of the cliff, he constructed two cisterns, and by digging into the rocks in many places made large reservoirs of water, so that the rain-water might collect, and the garrison might use it freely, and not be liable to capture through distress for want of water.

He also rebuilt solidly, and gave their present beauty and strength to all the other mountain forts, which reach from this point and from the city of Dara to Amida; namely, Ciphæ, Sauræ, Smargdis, Lurnes, Hieriphthon, Atachæ, Siphris, Rhipalthæ, Banasymeon, and also Sinæ, Rhasius, Dabanæ, and all the others which were built there in ancient times, and which before this were constructed in a contemptible fashion, but which he made into an impregnable line of outposts along the Roman frontier. In this region there stands a very lofty mountain, precipitous, and altogether inaccessible; the plain below it is rich and free from rocks, suitable both for arable and pasture land, for it abounds in grass. There are many villages at the foot of this mountain, whose inhabitants are rich in the produce of the country, but lie exposed to the attacks of the enemy. This was remedied by the Emperor Justinian, who built a fort upon the summit of the mountain, in which they might place their most valued possessions, and themselves take refuge at the approach of the enemy. This is named the Fort of the Emperors. Moreover, he carefully rebuilt and safely fortified the forts in the neighbourhood of the city of Amida, which before were only surrounded by mud walls, and were incapable of defence. Among these were Apadnæ and the little fort of Byrthum: for it is not easy to set down all their names in detail, but, speaking generally, he found them all exposed to attack, and has now rendered them impregnable; and since his time Mesopotamia has become quite protected against the Persian nation.

Nor must I pass over in silence what he devised at the fort of Bara, of which I just now spoke. The interior of this fort was entirely without water, and Bara is built upon the precipitous summit of a lofty mountain. Outside its walls, at a great distance, at the bottom of the hill, there was a fountain which it was not thought advisable to include within the fortification, lest the part which was situated upon the low ground should be open to attack. He therefore devised the following plan. He ordered them to dig within the walls until they reached the level of the plain. When this was done in accordance with the Emperor's order, to their surprise they found the water of the fountain flowing there; thus the fort was both constructed securely and conveniently situated with regard to water supply.

V. In the same manner, since the walls of Theodosiopolis,* the bulwark of the Roman Empire on the river Aborrhas, had become so decayed by age that the inhabitants derived no confidence from their strength, but rather terror, as they feared that before long they would fall down, the Emperor rebuilt them for the most part, so that they were able to check the invasions of the Persians into Mesopotamia. It is worth describing what he did at Constantina. The original wall of Constantina was so low that a ladder would easily reach the top, and in its construction was greatly exposed to attack, and seemed hardly to have been built in earnest; for the towers were of such a distance from one another, that if the assailants attacked the space between them, the garrison of the towers would be too far off to drive them back; moreover, the greater part of it was so ruinous from age that it seemed likely soon to fall. In addition to this, the city had an outwork which was more like a siege-work to enable the enemy to attack it; for it was not more than three feet in thickness, cemented with mud, the lower part of it built of rock fit for making mill-stones, but the

---

* Founded by Theodosius II. V. 'De Bello Persico,' i. 10.— Gibbon. (S.) Now probably Ras el 'Ain on the Khabûr. (W.)

upper part of what is called white-stone, which is not to be trusted and is very soft, so that the whole work might easily be captured. However, the Emperor Justinian rebuilt the decayed part of the walls, more especially on the west and north sides; between every two towers of the wall he placed the third, so that since his time all the towers for the defence of the wall stand close together. He also greatly raised the height of the wall and of all the towers, so as to render the place impregnable to an enemy. Moreover, he built covered approaches to the towers, each of which towers contained three stories of vaulted stone, so that each one of them was called and really was a castle in itself, for what the Greeks call 'phrourion' is called a 'castle' in the Latin tongue. Besides this, Constantina used formerly to be reduced to great straits for want of water; there are indeed wells of good water outside the walls at the distance of a mile, round which grows a large wood of very lofty trees; within the walls, however, since the streets are not built upon level but upon sloping ground, the city in ancient times was waterless, and its inhabitants suffered much from thirst and the difficulty of obtaining water; but the Emperor Justinian brought the water within the walls by means of an aqueduct, adorned the city with overflowing fountains, and may justly be termed its founder. These were the works of the Emperor Justinian in these cities.

VI. The Romans had a fort by the side of the river Euphrates on the extreme frontier of Mesopotamia, at the place where the river Aborrhas* effects its junction with the Euphrates. This fort was named Circesium,† and had

---

* River Aborrhas. The Chaboras at the juncture of the Khabûr and the Euphrates : the Chaboras of Ptolemy and Pliny and probably the Araxes of Xenophon ; now the Khabûr. (W.)

† 'Circesium, the last Roman station on the Euphrates.'—Gibbon, ch. xl. (S.) Now Kirkisiah at the juncture of the Khabûr and the Euphrates. (W.)

been built in former times by the Emperor Diocletian; however, our present Emperor Justinian, finding that it had become ruinous through lapse of time, and was neglected and not in a posture of defence, altered it into a strong fortification, and made it into a city of eminent size and beauty. When Diocletian built the fort he did not completely surround it with a wall, but brought each end of the walls down to the river Euphrates, built a tower at each end of them, and left the side between them entirely unfortified, imagining, I suppose, that the waters of the river would suffice to defend the fort on that side. In the course of time, however, the stream of the river, continually eating away the bank, undermined the tower on the south side, and it became evident that unless prompt measures were taken it would shortly fall. Now appeared the Emperor Justinian, entrusted by Heaven with the glory of watching over, and, as far as one man can do, of restoring the Roman Empire. He not only saved the undermined tower, which he rebuilt of a hard stone, but also enclosed all the unprotected side of the fort with a very strong wall, thus doubling its security by adding the strength which it derived from the wall to that afforded by the river. Besides this, he also built a powerful outwork round the city, especially at the spot where the junction of the two rivers forms a triangular space, and thus left no place exposed to the attacks of the enemy. Moreover, he appointed a general who had the title of Duke, and who always resided there with a garrison of picked soldiers, thus rendering the place a sufficient bulwark for the frontier of the empire. He also rebuilt in its present splendour the public bath which is used by the inhabitants, which had become quite ruinous and useless by the incursions of the river; for he found all that part of it which is suspended above the solid foundation for the convenience of bathers, underneath which the fire is placed, and which is called the hypocaust, exposed to the influx of the river, by which the bath was rendered useless ; he therefore strengthened with stonework, as I have said, the part which formerly had been hollow, and built another hypocaust above it, which the river could not reach, thus restoring the enjoyment of the bath to the garrison. In this manner did our Emperor restore the buildings of Circesium.

Beyond Circesium there is an ancient fort named Annucas, whose wall the Emperor Justinian found a mere ruin, and which he rebuilt in so magnificent a fashion that its defences vie with those of the most celebrated cities ; and in the same manner he rendered formidable, and altogether unapproachable by an enemy, those forts situated near the city of Theodosiopolis, which before his time were either without walls, or only walled with mud and absurd heaps of stones. These are Magdalathum, with two others on either side of it, and the two forts, the Great and Little Thannurium, Bismideon, Themeres, Bidamas, Dausaron. Thiolla, Philæ, Zamarthas, and, one may say, all the rest. There was an extensive position near Thannurium, which could easily be occupied by our enemies the Saracens, by crossing the river Aborrhas, from which point they were able to penetrate in small parties into the thick and extensive forest and the mountain which is situated in that region, and make inroads upon the Roman inhabitants of that country ; now, however, the Emperor Justinian has built a tower of hard stone in that place, manned it with a considerable garrison, and has altogether repressed the incursions of the enemy by the establishment of this bulwark against them.

VII. The above are the works of the Emperor Justinian in this part of Mesopotamia ; I must speak in this place of Edessa, Carrhæ, Callinicum, and all the other strong places which are in that country, since they lie between the two rivers. Edessa* stands on the banks of a small stream called Scirtus, which collects its waters from many places, and runs through the midst of the city: from thence it passes onwards, after having supplied the wants of the city, effecting its entrance and exit through by a channel constructed by former generations, which passes through the city walls. This river once, after much rain, rose to a great height, and seemed as though it would destroy the city; it tore down a large part of the outworks and of the walls, inundated almost the whole city, and did much damage, suddenly destroying the finest buildings, and drowning a third part of the inhabitants. The Emperor Justinian not only at once restored all the buildings of the city which were overthrown, among which were the

* 'La fortification byzantine se composait de plusieurs parties qui correspondent du *vallum, agger*, et *mœnium* des fortifications Romaines. C'est le τεῖχος, le mur ou la courtine, sur la face de laquelle s'élèvent les tours ; en avant de ce mur s'élève le mur du parapet, première defense de la courtine, προτείχισμα. Ce mur est espacé (du τεῖχος) de la courtine d'un quart environ de la hauteur totale. L'espace compris entre ces deux murs est le péribole (περίβολος), le chemin couvert. Ce mot est appliqué aussi au chemin interieur de l'agger qui longe le fossé (τάφρος). L'agger, qui se compose des terres du fossé, est soutenu par un mur, quelquefois flanqué de tours, qui est le ἀντιτείχισμα, mur de l'avant rempart. Les tours (πύργοι), sont appliquées a l'une et l'autre murailles. La courtine est surmontée d'un parapet. C'est la partie du remparts qui porte le nom de ἐπιτείχισμα, muraille supérieure : sur cette muraille sont placés les creneaux, ἐπάλξεις, qui sont quelquefois réunis par un mur dans la partie supérieure, et forment des espèces de barbacanes, θυρίδαι, pour lancer les traits. Le creneau etait quelquefois surmonté d'un pyramidion, d'autres fois il etait fendu par un encoche pour appuyer le trait.

'On ne saurait doubter que la ville d'Edesse n'eut été munie d'un double rempart ; car ces deux parties, προτείχισμα et περίβολος, sont specialement mentionnées par Procope dans la relation du siège d'Edesse. C'est la muraille extérieure, ἐκτὸς τεῖχος, qui soutient l'agger, et par conséquent forme le chemin couvert, ὁ μέγας περίβολος.'—Texier, 'Monographe sur l'Edesse.' (S.) It is now Urfa. (W.)

church of the Christians and a building called Antiphorus, but also arranged with great care that no such disaster should ever again occur, for he made a new channel for the river, outside the city walls, which he arranged in the following manner. The ground on the right bank of the river was formerly flat and low-lying, while that on the left was a precipitous mountain, which did not allow the river to turn aside from its accustomed course, but forced it to flow into the city, because when flowing towards the city it met with no obstacle on its right bank. He therefore dug away the whole of this mountain, making a channel on the left bank of the river deeper than its former bed, and built on the right bank an enormous wall of stones, as large as a waggon could carry, so that if the river ran as usual with a moderate volume the city would not be deprived of the convenience of its water; but if it should be swollen into a flood a moderate stream would run as usual throughout the city, but the excess of water would be forced into this channel constructed by Justinian, and thus extraordinarily conquered by human art and skill might run round the back of the race-course, which is situated not far off. Moreover he forced the river within the city to run in a straight course, by building a wall above it on either side, so that it could not turn out of a straight path; by which means he both preserved the use of it for the city, and removed all fear of it for the future. The wall and outwork of Edessa, like those of the other places, had for the most part fallen into ruins through age; wherefore the Emperor restored them both, making them new and much stronger than they were before. Part of the wall of Edessa is occupied by a fort, outside of which rises a hill very close to the city and overhanging it; this hill was in ancient times occupied by the inhabitants, and included in their walls by an outwork, that it might not form a weak point to the city. Their work, however, made the city much more open to assault in that quarter; for their outwork was very low, built on an exposed site, and could be taken even by children playing at sieges. Justinian therefore took it down and built another wall on the top of the hill, which is in no danger of an assault from higher ground in any quarter,

EDESSA.
From Texier & Pullan's Byzantine Architecture
COLUMNS ON A TERRACE OF THE CASTLE.

and which follows the slope of the hill down to the level ground on both sides, and joins the city wall.*

* 'The text (Procopius) is so conformable to the topography of the town, that it would appear to have been written on the spot.
'We do not find, near the banks of the river, any vestige of the hippodrome mentioned by Procopius in "De Bello Persico," book i., ch. xii. (L.)

Also at the cities of Carrhæ* and Callinicum† he destroyed the walls and outworks, which were much impaired by age, and rendered them impregnable by building the present complete fortifications; he also built a strong wall round the unprotected and neglected fort at Batnæ,‡ and gave it the fine appearance which it now presents.

VIII. These, as I have said before, were the works of the Emperor Justinian in Mesopotamia and Osrhoene. I will now describe what was done on the right bank of the river Euphrates. In all other parts the Roman and Persian frontiers border upon one another, and each nation proceeds from its own country to make war and peace with the other, as all men of different habits and empires do when they have a common frontier; but in the province which was formerly called Commagene, which is now called Euphratesia, they dwell nowhere near to one another, for the Roman and Persian frontiers are widely

---

'A stranger is struck by the imposing aspect of the ancient castle; the same which was constructed by Justinian. Its form is that of a parallelogram, 400 by 200 yards, defended by several square and two large semi-octagonal towers. The capitals of the two Corinthian columns are surmounted by blocks of stone which show that they were intended to have some further decoration—probably the statues of Justinian and Theodora.—The diameter of each column is nearly two yards.'—Texier and Pullan, pp. 181-184.

'In Smith's "Dict. of Geog.," it is stated that as late as 1184, there were fifteen large churches, which fell into the hands of the Saracens. It was deserted in 1285.

* Carrhæ (now Harran), a few miles south of Edessa.

† Callinicum, on the Euphrates, and marked on the map as 'or Nicephorium,' at the junction with the river Bilecha (Bilek). (L.)

‡ 'On voit que l'historien Grec donne indistinctement à cette place les noms de Βάτνη au singulier, et Βάτναι au pluriel. . . . La table de Peutinger donne le nom Batna. Ce qui m'a surtout frappé dans cette localité, ce sont les vastes carrières qui ont dû fournir à une exploitation considérable. Une grande partie des matériaux qui ont servi aux constructions d'Edesse en à sans doute été tirée.'—'Edesse et ses Monuments,' par Ch. Texier, Membre de l'Institut, Paris, 1859. (S.)

parted by a country which is quite desert and devoid of life, and possesses nothing worth fighting for. Yet each nation, though not regarding it as a work of much importance, has built a chain of forts of unbaked brick where the desert borders upon their inhabited country. None of these forts have ever been assaulted by their neighbours, but the two nations dwell there without any ill-feeling, since there is nothing for either of them to covet; however, the Emperor Diocletian built three of these forts in this desert, one of which, named Mambri, had fallen into ruin through age, and was restored by the Emperor Justinian.

About five miles from this fort, as you go towards the Roman country, Zenobia, the wife of Odenathus, the chief of the Saracens in those parts, built a small city in former times and gave it her own name, calling it Zenobia.* Since then, long lapse of time brought its walls to ruin, and as the Romans did not think it worth caring for, it became entirely uninhabited. Thus the Persians, whenever they chose, were able to place themselves in the midst of the Romans before any news had been heard of their coming; however, the Emperor Justinian rebuilt the whole of Zenobia, filled it with numerous inhabitants, placed in it a commander with a garrison of regular soldiers, and thus formed a powerful fortress, a bulwark of the Roman Empire and a check upon the Persians. He did not merely restore it to its former appearance, but made it far stronger than it was before. The place is closely surrounded by high cliffs, from which the enemy were formerly

* 'The ruins present the form of an acute triangle, having its base resting on the river, whilst its sides climb the acclivity of a conical hill, and terminate at its summit in a small Acropolis. It was defended by walls flanked by strong towers, which, as well as the public and private buildings, were all constructed of fine gypsum (which abounds along the Euphrates), and are as sharp and fresh as if they had recently been built.'—' Narrative of the Euphrates Expedition,' p. 247, by F. R. Chesney, London, 1868. 8vo. (L.)

able to shoot down upon the heads of the defenders of the wall; being desirous to avoid this, he constructed a building upon the walls, on the side nearest these cliffs, which might always act as a protection to the defenders. This building is called a 'wing,' because it appears to hang upon the wall. Indeed, it is not possible to describe all that our Emperor built at Zenobia: for as the city is situated far away in the desert, and for this reason is always exposed to peril, and cannot derive any succour from the Romans, who dwell at a distance, he took the greatest pains to render it secure. I will now relate some few of his works there.

Zenobia stands beside the river Euphrates, which flows close to its walls on the eastern side. This river, surrounded by high mountains, has no space in which to extend itself, but its stream is confined among the neighbouring mountains and between its rugged banks. Whenever it is swollen by rain into a flood, it pours against the city wall and washes not merely against its foundations but as high as its very battlements. The courses of stone in the walls, drenched by this stream, became disarranged, and the whole construction was endangered; he, however, constructed a mole of enormous masses of hard rock, of the same length as the wall, and forced the flooded river to expend its rage in vain, setting the wall free from any fear of injury, however high the river might swell. Finding that the city wall upon the northern side had become ruinous from age, he razed it to the ground, together with its outwork, and rebuilt it, but not upon its former site, because the houses of the city were so crowded together at that point as to inconvenience the inhabitants; but he proceeded beyond the foundations of the wall, beyond the outwork and the ditch itself, and there built an admirable and singularly beautiful wall, thus greatly enlarging

Zenobia in this quarter. There was, moreover, a certain hill which stood near the city towards the west, from which the barbarians, when they made their attacks, were able to shoot with impunity down upon the heads of the defenders, and even of those who were standing in the midst of the city; this hill the Emperor Justinian surrounded with a wall on both sides, and thus included it in the city of Zenobia, afterwards escarping its sides throughout, so that no enemy could ascend it. He also built another fort upon the top of the hill, and thus rendered it altogether inaccessible to those who wished to assault the city, for beyond the hill the ground sinks into a hollow valley, and therefore it cannot be closely approached by the enemy; above this hollow valley the mountains at once rise on the western side. The Emperor did not merely watch over the safety of the city, but also built churches in it, and barracks for the soldiers: he also constructed public baths and porticos. All this work was carried out under the superintendence of the architects Isidorus and Joannes, of whom Joannes was a Byzantine, and Isidorus a Milesian by birth, being the nephew of that Isidorus whom I mentioned before. Both of these were young men, but showed an energy beyond their years, and both displayed equal zeal in the works which they constructed for the Emperor.

IX. After Zenobia was the city of Suri,* situated on the river Euphrates, whose fortifications were so contemptible that when Chosroes assaulted it, it did not hold out for so much as half-an-hour, but was instantly taken by the Persians. This fort, however, like Callinicum, was restored by the Emperor Justinian, who surrounded it with a strong wall, strengthened it with an outwork, and enabled it for the future to resist the attack of the enemy,

* Súri (now Surieh), a few miles west of Callinicum. (W.)

There is in Euphratesia a church dedicated to Sergius, an eminent saint, whom the ancients so admired and looked up to that they named the place Sergiopolis,* and surrounded it with a low rampart, sufficient to prevent the Saracens in that region from capturing it by assault; for the Saracens are by nature incapable of attacking walls, and consequently the weakest mud wall is sufficient to resist their onset. In later times this church received so many offerings as to become powerful and famous throughout the land. The Emperor Justinian, reflecting upon these matters, at once applied himself to its protection, surrounded it with a most admirable wall, and provided a quantity of water, stored up in reservoirs, for the use of its inhabitants; besides this, he built in the place houses and porticos, and all the other buildings which are regarded as the ornaments of a city. He also placed a garrison of soldiers in it to defend the walls in time of need; and, indeed, Chosroes, the King of Persia, who determined to take the city, and who brought up a large army to besiege it, was compelled to raise the siege, being overcome by the strength of the walls.

The Emperor spent equal care upon all the towns and forts on the borders of Euphratesia, (namely) Barbalissus,† Neocæsarea, Gabula, Pentacomia, which is on the Euphrates, and Europus.‡ At Hemerius, finding the walls built in some parts carelessly and dangerously, and in some parts formed only of mud, while the place was deficient in water-supply and consequently despicable as a fortification, he razed them to the ground, and at once carefully rebuilt them of courses of the hardest stone, making the wall

* Is this the same as Tetrapyrgia, where St. Sergius was buried? (W.)

† Barbalissus (now Kala), at Balis, on the Euphrates. See Ant. Mart., 'Itin.,' xlvii. (W.)

‡ On the Euphrates, now probably Jerablûs, supposed by some to be the site of Carchemish. (W.)

much wider and higher than before. He also constructed reservoirs for water in all parts of the works, all of which he filled with rain-water, and, placing a garrison there, he rendered the place as powerful and secure as we now see it. Indeed, if one were carefully to consider this, and to inspect all the other good works of the Emperor Justinian, one would say it was for this alone that he had received the crown, by the manifest favour of God, who watches over the Roman people.

Besides these places he also found Hierapolis,* which is the chief of all the cities in that region, lying exposed to any enemy that might attack it, but by his own provident foresight he rendered it safe; for, as it originally enclosed a large empty space and on that account the entire circuit of the walls could not be guarded, he cut off the part which was useless, arranged the walls in a safer and more compact form, and, by thus reducing it to the size necessary for use, made it one of the strongest cities of the present day. He also conferred upon it the following benefit. A fountain of sweet water springs perpetually out of the earth in the midst of the city, and forms therein a

* Hierapolis (Bambych), formerly the capital of Euphratesia, on west of Euphrates, between Antioch and Edessa. 'Has no records of its ancient greatness but its walls, which may be traced all round; cannot be less than three miles in compass . . . with towers of large square stone, extremely well built. A deep pit of about 100 yards diameter seemed to have had great buildings all round it, with the pillars and ruins of which it is now in part filled up, but not so much but that there was still water in it. Here are a multitude of subterraneous aqueducts brought to this city. You can ride nowhere about the city without seeing them.'—Maundrell's 'Journey from Aleppo to Euphrates,' Bohn's edition, 8vo., p. 507, 1848. (L.)

Hierapolis (Bambij, or Membij). The whole place is now a mass of ruin, but the outlines of a theatre and stadium can be traced. The lake is now represented by a deep circular pool, said to be always full of water. There are several springs in the ruins, and water was also supplied by 'Kariz,' or underground channels. Formerly a centre of great commercial importance; our word 'bombazine' comes from Bambya. (W., MS. notes, 1881.)

wide lake; this, indeed, added to the safety of the city when it was beleaguered by an enemy, but in time of peace was by no means necessary, as much water was brought into the city from without. In process of time the inhabitants, having enjoyed a long period of peace, and having never experienced any distress, neglected this spring; for it is not in human nature when in prosperity to make provision against times of adversity; consequently they gradually filled up the lake with rubbish, and were accustomed to bathe in it, to wash their clothes in it, and to throw all kinds of refuse into it. . . .

In this province of Euphratesia were situated two other towns, Zeugma* and Neocæsarea, which were indeed towns in name, but were merely surrounded by dry stone walls, built so low that they might be crossed by an enemy without any difficulty, since they could leap over them without fear; while they were so narrow as to be altogether indefensible, because they afforded no room for the garrison to stand upon to defend them; however, the Emperor Justinian surrounded these places also with real walls, of a sufficient width and height, and equipped them with all other means of defence, thus giving them a just right to be termed cities, and rendering them safe from the attacks of the enemy.

X. Moreover, with regard to the cities taken from Chosroes, that barbarian, disregarding the perpetual peace which he had sworn to observe, and the money which he had received on account of it, was filled with envy of the Emperor Justinian, because of the conquests which he had made in Libya and in Italy, and considered his plighted faith to be of less importance than the gratification of this passion; he watched his opportunity, when the greater part of the Roman army was away in the West, and invaded the Roman territory unexpectedly,

* Zeugma, on the right bank of the Euphrates, opposite Biredjik. (W.)

before the Romans had any news of the approach of the enemy; these cities, I say, the Emperor Justinian so strengthened and beautified that they are all at the present time much more flourishing than before, and have no dread of injury from barbarian invasion, fearing no attacks of any kind.

Above all, he rendered the city of Antiochia,* which is now surnamed Theopolis, far more beautiful and powerful than it was before; its wall in ancient times was too large, and extended beyond all reason, uselessly enclosing flat ground in one place, and lofty cliffs in another, so that it was full of weak points. The Emperor Justinian reduced it to a useful size, making it protect the city alone, and not the places which it formerly enclosed. In the lower part of the fortifications, where the city had spread out to a dangerous extent over a smooth plain, and was indefensible through the great length of the wall, he drew it back as far as possible, advantageously reducing

---

* Antiochia, now Antâkieh, founded by Seleucus Nicator. Having been nearly ruined by an earthquake it was almost rebuilt by Justinian, and called by him Theodopolis. In A.D. 1163, it is described by Benjamin of Tudela as a large city very strongly fortified, 'overlooked by a very high mountain; a wall surrounds this height, on the summit of which is situated a well. The inspector of the well distributes the water by subterranean aqueducts, and thus provides the houses of the principal inhabitants of the city. The other side of the city is surrounded by the river.' A plan of the city is given under 'Antioch' in Smith's 'Dict. of Antiquities.'

'The city (the modern Antakieh) covers but a small part of the ground occupied by the ancient city, though it still contains fourteen mosques.

'The population in 1836 was under 6,000.

'The walls of the ancient city are comparatively perfect.

'From the Acropolis the wall has been carried down the almost vertical face of the cliff, and after crossing the valley, is made to ascend the opposite steep hill in a zigzag and extraordinary manner.

'At the steepest part of the hills these walls necessarily become a succession of gigantic steps between the towers, which, at some places, are close to one another.'—'Narrative of the Euphrates Expedition,' p. 189, by J. R. Chesney, London, 1868. (L.)

the size of the city in that quarter, and strengthening it by concentration. As for the river Orontes, which formerly flowed past it in a circuitous course, he changed its direction, and caused it to skirt the walls of the city. Thus, by an artificial channel, he brought the course of the river as near the city as possible, by which means he relieved the city from the danger of its unmanageable size, and yet retained the protection afforded by the river Orontes: then, by building new bridges, he supplied fresh means of intercourse across the river, which he diverted from its course as far as was required, and then returned to its former bed.

The upper part of the city, on the high ground, he fortified in the following manner. On the summit of the mountain which is called Orocassias there is a lofty rock which stands close outside the wall opposite to the fortifications in that quarter, and which renders them easy to attack. It was from this point that Chosroes took the city, as I have explained in my work on the subject. The region within the walls was for the most part uninhabited and difficult of access, for the place is divided by lofty rocks and deep ravines, which cut off all the paths, so that the wall of Antiochia seems there to belong to another city. He therefore disregarded the rock which overhangs the wall so close and renders it liable to capture, and decided to build his new wall at a distance from it, having learnt by experience the folly of the original builders; moreover, he levelled the ground within the walls, which formerly had been precipitous, and made the ascent to this part of the city not only practicable for people on foot, but for horsemen and even for carriages. On this high ground he also built baths and reservoirs for water within the walls, and dug a well in each tower, remedying the original waterless character of the place by the storage of rain-water.

It is worth our while to describe his works upon the torrent which descends from these mountains. Two precipitous mountains overhang the city, standing close to one another; of these, the one is called Orocassias, the other Stauris. They are joined by a glen and ravine which lies between them, which in time of rain produces the torrent named Onopnictes, which used to flow down from the high ground and overflow the fortifications, and sometimes rose so high as to pour into the streets of the city, doing much mischief to the inhabitants. The Emperor Justinian remedied this in the following manner. In front of that part of the wall which is nearest to the ravine, from which the torrent used to rush against the wall, he built an exceedingly high wall, reaching from the hollow bed of the ravine to the mountains on either side, so that the torrent was not able to rush past it, but was forced to stay and collect its waters there. In this wall he made apertures, through which he forced the water to run gently in a smaller volume, checked by this artificial barrier, so that it no longer broke with its full force against the city wall so as to overflow it and ruin the city, but proceeded gently and quietly, as I have explained, and flowing in this manner passed wherever it was desired to go through the channels constructed for it by the former inhabitants.

Thus did the Emperor Justinian reconstruct the walls of Antiochia; he also rebuilt the entire city, which was burnt by the enemy. As the whole city was reduced to ashes, and levelled to the ground, and only heaps of rubbish remained after the conflagration, it was at first impossible for the citizens of Antiochia to recognise the site of their own dwellings. He consequently removed all the ruins, and cleared away the charred remains of the houses; but, as there were no public porticos or halls supported by columns, no market-place, and no streets which marked out the quarters of the city, there was nothing to point to the site of any particular house. However, the Emperor, without any delay, removed the rubbish as far as possible from the city, thus freeing the air and the ground from all impediments to building, and first covered the foundations of the city everywhere with stones large enough to load a waggon. After this he divided it by porticos and market-places, defined all the blocks of building by streets, arranged the aqueducts, fountains, and watercourses with which the city is adorned, constructed theatres and public baths in it, and graced it with all the other public buildings which belong to a prosperous city.

He also brought thither a number of workmen and artificers, and thus rendered it more easy for the inhabitants to rebuild their own houses; the result of this is that Antiochia at the present day is a more celebrated city than before. He also built therein a large church in honour of the Virgin, the beauty and magnificence of which is in all respects beyond description. He endowed this church with a considerable revenue, and also built a large church dedicated to St. Michael the Archangel. Moreover, he made provision for the sick poor in that place, and built dwellings for them, separate for the different sexes, in which they were supplied with attendants, and the means of curing their diseases; while at the same time he established hospices for strangers who might be staying for any time in the city.

XI. In like manner he also restored, greatly strengthened, and brought into its present condition the wall of the city of Chalcis, together with its outwork, which had become weak and ruinous through age.

There was in Syria an utterly neglected village named Cyrus,* which the Jews had built in ancient times when

---

* 'Cyrus, dans la Syrie. Procope rapporte que celle ville fut fondée par les Juifs. C'est la ville Cyrrhus de Ptolemée dont il fait la

they were led captive from Palestine into Syria by the army of the Medes, from which country they were long afterwards released by Cyrus the King; wherefore they called the place Cyrus in honour of their benefactor. In the course of time Cyrus became quite overlooked and was entirely without walls; but the Emperor Justinian, with a prudent zeal for the safety of the Empire, and also out of reverence for the SS. Cosmas and Damianus, whose bodies lay near that place down to my own time, made Cyrus into a flourishing and admirable city, rendering it safe by a very strong wall, with a numerous garrison, large public buildings, and with all other appurtenances on an exceedingly magnificent scale. In former times the interior of this city was without water, but outside the walls was a plenteous spring which provided abundance of drinking-water, yet was altogether useless to the inhabitants, since they had no means of drawing water from it without great labour and peril; for they were obliged to go to it by a circuitous path, as the country between it and the city was precipitous and altogether impassable, so that an enemy, if he were present, could easily lay an ambush and cut them off. He therefore constructed a watercourse from the city walls to the fountain, not open, but concealed underground with the greatest care, which supplied the city with water without either trouble or danger.

He also very strongly rebuilt the entire circuit of the walls of Chalcis,* which had fallen into ruin down to its

---

capitale de la Cyrrhestique. Elle était à 2 journées d'Antioche. Ou la nomme aussi Cyrrhus.'—'Encyclopédie Méthodique,' 'Géographie Ancienne,' Paris, 1787. (L.) It is now Chorres, north-west of Aleppo. (W.)

* 'Chalcis, between Beyrout and Damascus, where there are ruins of the old city, surrounded by a prostrate wall. Two or three miserable hovels are now the only representatives of a royal city.'—Porter's (Murray's) 'Syria and Palestine,' 1875, p. 515. (L.) Is not the Northern Chalcis (now Kinnesrin), south-west of Aleppo, intended? It is mentioned in 'Itin.,' Ant., also in Ant. Mart., 'Itin.' (W.)

very foundation and was altogether indefensible, and he strengthened it with an outwork; he also restored all the other towns and forts in Syria in an admirable fashion.

Thus did the Emperor Justinian provide for the security of Syria; there is, too, in Phœnicia, by the side of Lebanon, a city named Palmyra, which was built in the desert in ancient times, and which was conveniently placed on the road by which our enemies the Saracens would enter our country. It was, indeed, originally built for this purpose; namely, in order to prevent the barbarians making unexpected inroads into the Roman territory. This place, which through lapse of time had become almost entirely deserted, was strongly fortified by the Emperor Justinian, who supplied it abundantly with water, and filled it with a garrison of soldiers, so as to check the inroads of the Saracens.

BOOK III.

I. THE Emperor Justinian fortified the eastern country in the manner which I have described in a former part of this work. Now as I started from the Persian frontier in my description of his work upon the fortresses, I think it will be convenient to proceed from thence to that of Armenia, which skirts the Persian territory from the city of Amida as far as that of Theodosiopolis. Before describing the buildings in that quarter, I think it would be advisable to give some account of how our Emperor brought the Armenians out of a condition of danger and terror into their present state of settled security; for he did not preserve these his subjects by buildings alone, but also by his foresight in other matters, as I shall presently explain. To do this I must refer for a short time to ancient history.

In old times the Armenians had a king of their own nation, as we are told by the historians of remotest antiquity. When, however, Alexander of Macedon overthrew the King of Persia, the Persians remained quiet under his yoke, but the Parthians revolted against the Macedonians, conquered them in war, drove them out of their country, and pushed their frontier as far as the river Tigris. Subsequently the Persians remained subject to them for five hundred years, up to the time when Alexander, the son of Mamæa, ruled over the Romans. At this time one of the kings of the Parthians made his brother, named Arsaces, King of the Armenians, as the history of the Armenians tells us; for let no one suppose that the Arsacidæ are Armenians. Now for five hundred years there was peace between them in consequence of their relationship. The King of the Armenians dwelt in what is called Greater Armenia, having been from ancient times subject to the Emperor of the Romans; but afterwards one Arsaces, King of Armenia, had two sons, named Tigranes and Arsaces. When this King was about to die, he made a will by which he left the succession to his kingdom to both his sons, not dividing its power equally between them, but giving a fourfold greater share to Tigranes. The elder Arsaces, after making this division of his kingdom, passed away, but Arsaces his son, grieved and enraged at the inferiority of his position, laid the matter before the Roman Empire, hoping that by using all means in his power he might drive his brother from the kingdom, and render his father's unjust wishes of no effect. At this time Theodosius, the son of Arcadius, ruled over the Romans, being still a child. Tigranes, fearing the Emperor's vengeance, put himself in the hands of the Persians and handed over his kingdom to them, preferring to live as a private man amongst the Persians, rather than to make an equitable arrangement with his brother, and rule jointly over the Armenians with him in good faith and honour. Arsaces, being equally afraid of the attacks of the Persians and of his brother, abdicated his own kingdom in favour of the Emperor Theodosius, on certain conditions, which I have explained at length in my History of the Wars. For some time the country of the Armenians was an object of contention between the Romans and the Persians, but they finally agreed that the Persians should possess the share of Tigranes, and the Romans that of Arsaces. Both parties signed a treaty on these conditions, and henceforth the Emperor of the Romans appointed whom he pleased, and at what time he thought proper, to rule over the Armenians. This ruler was called the Count of Armenia down to my own time.

However, since such a kingdom as this was not capable of repelling the incursions of the enemy, because it possessed no regular army, the Emperor Justinian, perceiving that Armenia was always in a disorderly condition, and therefore was an easy prey to the barbarians, put an end to this form of government, and placed a general in command of the Armenians, giving him a sufficient number of regular soldiers to repel the invasions of the enemy. This was the arrangement which he adopted for what is called Greater Armenia; but the remainder of Armenia, that which reaches from this side of the river Euphrates as far as the city of Amida, was governed by five Armenian satraps, whose offices were hereditary and tenable for life; however, they received the insignia of their office from the hands of the Roman Emperor alone. It is worth while to explain what these insignia were, since they will never again be seen by men: they were a cloak made of wool, not such as grows on sheep, but such as is gathered from the sea. The animal on whom this wool grows is called 'pinna.' The cloak was of purple, covered with gold at that part where it was fastened together; there was a gold brooch upon the cloak, containing a precious stone, from which three amethysts were suspended by loose golden chains. The tunic was of silk, entirely covered with the golden ornaments known as 'feather-work;' the boots were red-coloured, reaching to the knee, such as it is not lawful for anyone to wear except the Roman Emperors and the Kings of Persia.

No Roman soldiers were ever employed either by the King of Armenia or the satraps, but they trusted exclusively to their own resources in war. In later times, however, during the reign of the Emperor Zeno, when Illus and Leontius openly revolted against the Emperor, certain of the satraps took their side; wherefore the Emperor Zeno, after his victory over Illus and Leontius, allowed one of the satraps, whose satrapy—that of the country called Belabitis—was the weakest and least important, to retain his former possession, but deposed all the others, and did not allow these governments any longer to be held by hereditary descent, but filled them by persons chosen by the Emperor, as is the custom with all the other Roman governments. Yet even then Roman soldiers were not placed in them, but Armenian soldiers, as had formerly been customary, and who were quite unable to defend them against the attacks of the enemy. Perceiving this, the Emperor Justinian abolished the title of satrap for all time to come, and appointed two rulers over these nations, with the title of Dukes, giving them a large number of regular Roman soldiers, in order that with them they might defend the Roman frontier. He also built for them strong places, as follows.

II. I shall begin with the country of Mesopotamia, in order to connect my account with what has been described above. He established one of these rulers of the Armenian tribes, who have the title of Duke, in the city which is called Martyropolis,* and the other in a fortress which is named Citharizon. I will now describe in what part of the Roman Empire these places are situated. The city of Martyropolis is situated in that part of Armenia which is called Sophanene, close to the river Nymphius, and bordering closely on the enemy's country; for at that place the river Nymphius divides the Roman and Persian territory. Beyond the river lies the country named Arxanes, which from ancient times has belonged to the Persians. Yet this city was always neglected by the Romans, and lay exposed to the attacks of these barbarians; so that Cabades, the King of the Persians, in the reign of the Emperor Anastasius, invaded the country of the Romans, and led an army through Martyropolis, which is distant from Amida a little more than a day's journey for a lightly equipped traveller. As a mere incident and unimportant part of his invasion he took this city without any siege, assault, or beleaguerment, but simply by giving out that he was coming; for the inhabitants, who knew well that they could not hold out for a single moment of time against his army, as soon as they saw the Median host near at hand, at once went over to Cabades, with Theodorus—who at that time was satrap of Sophanene—at their head, dressed in the insignia of his office, and delivered themselves and the city of Martyropolis up to him, taking with them the public revenue for two years. Cabades, pleased with this, refrained from

* 'Martyropolis, near the River Nymphæus. Tradition says that it was founded towards the end of the fifth century by Bishop Maroutha, who there collected the relics of all the martyrs which could be found in Armenia, Persia and Syria. It was the capital of Roman Armenia, now Miafarékyr.'— Smith's 'Dict. of Geography.' (L.)

ravaging the city and the entire country, which he regarded as part of the Persian Empire. He dismissed the people unhurt, and neither did any injury to them nor altered anything in their city, but replaced Theodorus—whom he regarded as a wise man—as satrap over them, placing in his hands the symbols of authority, and trusting him to protect the Persian territory. After this he led his army onwards, took Amida by a siege, and retired into the Persian territory, as I have described in my 'History of the Wars.' The Emperor Anastasius, perceiving that it was not possible for the city of Martyropolis to defend itself without any fortifications against the attacks of the enemy, not only was not angry with Theodorus and the people of Sophanene, but declared that he was very thankful to them for their action. The wall of the city of Martyropolis was in thickness about four feet, and in height about twenty feet; so that it could not only be easily captured by an enemy, who employed siege operations and brought battering engines against it, but could easily be escaladed.

In consequence of this, the Emperor Justinian proceeded as follows. He dug a trench outside the walls, laid foundations in it, and built a new wall of a thickness of four feet, at a distance of four feet from the old wall. He raised this wall also to a height of twenty feet, making it in all respects equal in size to the old one; he then filled up the space between the two walls with stones and mortar, thus forming the whole work into one wall twelve feet in thickness. He then raised it, keeping the thickness the same, to a height twice as great as that which it formerly possessed; moreover, he built an admirable outwork round the city, and built all the other defences of a fortified place.

III. On the west side of Martyropolis is a place named

Phison, which also is situated in that part of Armenia which is called Sophanene, and is distant from Martyropolis a little more than one day's journey. About eight miles beyond this place lie precipitous and altogether impassable mountains, between which are two narrow passes, situated close to one another, which are called Clisuræ. Travellers from Persian Armenia to Sophanene, whether they proceed from the Persian territory or by way of the fortress of Citharizon, must necessarily proceed through these two passes, of which the one is called by the natives Illyrisis, and the other Saphchæ. Each of these ought to be fortified with the utmost care, in order to bar the way against the enemy; in former times, however, they remained entirely unguarded. But the Emperor Justinian, by placing admirable fortifications both at Phison and in the passes, and by establishing sufficient garrisons in them, rendered it altogether impossible for the barbarians to invade the country. These were the works of the Emperor Justinian in that part of the country of Armenia which is called Sophanene.

In Citharizon, which is in the province called Asthianene, he built a new fort on a hilly spot, of great size, and completely impregnable. This place he furnished with a sufficient supply of water, and all other conveniences for its inhabitants, and placed in command of it, as I said before, the other Duke of Armenia with a sufficient garrison of soldiers, thus rendering the tribes of Armenia secure in this quarter also.

As one goes from Citharizon* towards Theodosiopolis and Greater Armenia is the country of Corzane, which extends for a distance of about three days' journey, without any lake, river or mountain to divide it from the country of the Persians, whose frontier is confused with it; so that the inhabitants of this region, whether they be Roman or

* Citharizon, now probably Pâlû on the Murad Chai. (W.)

Persian subjects, have no fear of one another, and never expect any attack, but intermarry with one another, have common markets for their produce, and cultivate the country together. When the rulers of either nation make an expedition against the other at the command of their prince, they always find their neighbours unprotected; for each of them has extremely populous places close to one another, while in former times there was no fortification whatever; so that it was possible for the King of Persia to invade the Roman territory in this quarter more easily than anywhere else, until the Emperor Justinian prevented his doing so, in the following manner. In the midst of this country there was a place named Artaleson, which he surrounded with a very strong wall, and made into an impregnable fortress; he placed a garrison of regular soldiers in it, and appointed a general over them, whom the Romans in the Latin language style 'a Duke.' Thus did he fortify the whole of that frontier.

IV. These were the works of the Emperor Justinian in that quarter. I now come to what he did in the rest of Armenia. The city of Satala was formerly in a perilous position, because it is not far distant from the enemy's country, and is built upon low ground, surrounded by many hills, so that it ought in consequence of its position to possess impregnable fortifications. However, its defences were even more untrustworthy than its position, the works having been badly and carelessly constructed, and by lapse of time having fallen into ruin. The whole of these were demolished by the Emperor, who built a new wall round it of sufficient height to appear to overtop the neighbouring hills, and of sufficient thickness to support such an unusual height with safety. He built round it an outwork of an admirable character, and struck despair into the heart of the enemy. He also built a very strong fort not far from Satala, in the province of Osrhoene.

In this province there was an old fort built by the ancients upon the ridge of a precipitous hill, which was once taken by Pompeius, the Roman general, who, when he became master of the country, fortified it with great care, and named it Colonia. The Emperor Justinian exerted all his power in restoring this fort, which had fallen into decay after so long a time; moreover, he distributed enormous sums of money among the inhabitants of this region, and thus persuaded them to build new fortifications on their own ground, and to restore those which had fallen into ruin; so that nearly all the works situated in that country were built by the Emperor Justinian. There also he built the forts of Baiberdon and Arcon; he restored Lysiormum and Lutararizon;* he also built a new fort in the place which is called the Ditch of Germanus. Moreover, he restored the walls of Sebastia† and Nicopolis, which are cities of Armenia, which were on the point of falling, having become decayed through age. In them he built churches and monasteries. At Theodosiopolis he built a church dedicated to the Virgin, and restored the monasteries in the places named Petrius and Cucarizon. At Nicopolis‡ he built the monastery of the Forty-five saints, and a church of St. George the Martyr at Bizana. Near Theodosiopolis he restored the monastery named after the Forty Martyrs.

There was a place in what used to be called Lesser Armenia, not far from the river Euphrates, where formerly a regiment of Roman soldiers was stationed. The place

* Q.y. Autararizon.

† 'Sebastia (Sivas) regarded by Pliny as not belonging to Pontus, but to Cappadocia. Its ancient name is unknown. Pompey increased it, and called it Megalopolis. Its walls were restored by Justinian: (Procopius). There are ruins of two castles of different epochs. One appears to have belonged to the kings of Pontus, strengthened by Romans and rebuilt by Mohammedans.'—Ainsworth's 'Journey' in Chesney, p. 529. (L.)

‡ Nicopolis now Shabhin Kara Hissar. (W)

was named Melitene, and the regiment was named Legion. Here the Romans in former times had built a square fortification on low ground, which was convenient for soldiers' quarters and for the reception of their standards. Afterwards, by the orders of Trajan, the Roman Emperor, the place was raised to the dignity of a city, and became the capital of that nation. In the course of time the city of Melitene became large and populous; and since it was no longer possible for the inhabitants to dwell within the fortification, which, as I have said, enclosed but a small space of ground, they built their city in the plain near it, erecting thereon their churches, the dwellings of their magistrates, the market-place, and the shops of their merchants, the streets, porticos, baths, theatres, and all the other ornaments of a large city. In this manner Melitene became for the most part composed of suburbs. The Emperor Anastasius attempted to enclose the whole of it with a wall, but died before he had carried out his intention; however, the Emperor Justinian built a wall all round it, and rendered Melitene* a great defence and ornament to the Armenians.

V. These are the works of our Emperor in that part of Armenia which lies on the right bank of the Euphrates; I will now speak of what he did in Greater Armenia. When the Roman Emperor Theodosius obtained the kingdom of Arsaces, as I explained before, he built a castle on one of its hills, very liable to capture, which he called Theodosiopolis. This was taken by Cabades, the king of Persia, when he passed it as he was marching straight upon Amida. Not long afterwards the Roman Emperor Anastasius built a city there, enclosing within its walls the hill upon which Theodosius had placed his castle. Although he named the city after himself, yet he was not able to abolish the name of Theodosius, its former

* Melitene now Malatia. (W.)

founder; for though the things in common use among mankind are constantly changing, yet it is not easy to alter their former names. The wall of Theodosiopolis was of a sufficient width, but was not raised to a proportional height, for it was only about thirty feet high, and therefore was very liable to capture by an enemy skilled in sieges, such as the Persians. It was weak in other respects also, for it was not defended by any outwork or ditch; moreover, some high ground close to the city overhung the wall. These defects the Emperor Justinian remedied in the following manner; in the first place he dug a very deep trench all round it, like the bed of a torrent among precipitous mountains: next, he cut up the overhanging hill into a mass of inaccessible precipices and pathless ravines; moreover, in order to make the wall very high, and unassailable by an enemy, he employed the same device as at the city of Dara. He contracted the battlements to the smallest size through which it was possible to shoot at the besiegers, laid stones over them so as to make another story round the entire circuit, and skilfully placed a second set of battlements upon it, enclosing the whole place within an outwork like that of the city of Dara, and making each tower into a strong castle. He established in this place all the forces of Armenia, with their general, and rendered the Armenians so strong that they no longer feared the attacks of the Persians.

At Bizana the Emperor did nothing of this sort; for this place is situated upon flat country, surrounded by wide plains fit for the manœuvres of cavalry, and full of putrid pools of stagnant water; so that it was very easily stormed by an enemy, and was very unhealthy for its inhabitants; for these reasons, he neglected this place, and built a city elsewhere to which he gave his own name. It is a fine city and altogether impregnable, and stands in a place called Tzumina, distant three miles from Bizana, in a very healthy and airy position on high ground.

VI. These were the acts of the Emperor Justinian in Armenia. At this point of my narrative it appears convenient to describe what he did among the tribes of the Tzani, since they dwell next to the Armenians. In ancient times the Tzani were independent and without any rulers, living after the manner of wild beasts, regarding and worshipping as gods the woods and birds and other animals. They spent all their lives in lofty and thickly wooded mountains, and never cultivated the ground, but supported themselves by plundering and brigandage; for they themselves were unacquainted with agriculture, and their country, when it is not covered with precipitous mountains, is hilly: and the surface of these hills is not earthy, or capable of growing crops even if it were cultivated, but rough and hard, and altogether sterile. It is not possible to irrigate the ground, to reap a crop, or to find a meadow anywhere; and even the trees, with which the land of the Tzani is covered, bear no fruit, because for the most part there is no regular succession of seasons, and the land is not at one time subjected to cold and wet, and at another made fertile by the warmth of the sun, but is desolated by perpetual winter and covered by eternal snows. For this reason the Tzani, in ancient times, remained independent; but during the reign of our Emperor Justinian they were conquered by the Romans, under the command of Tzita; and, perceiving that resistance was impossible, at once submitted in a body, preferring an easy servitude to a dangerous freedom. They at once all changed their religion to the true faith, became Christians, and embraced a more civilized mode of life, renouncing brigandage, and serving in the Roman army, which was constantly at war with their enemies. However, the Emperor Justinian, fearing that the Tzani might at some time revert to their former wild mode of life, devised the following expedients.

The whole country of the Tzani is difficult, and quite impassable for horsemen, being everywhere surrounded with precipices and woods, as I said before; so that it was impossible for the Tzani to mix with their neighbours, but they lived by themselves in a savage manner, like wild beasts. He therefore cut down all the trees which hindered the making of roads, and levelled the rough ground, rendering it easily passable for horsemen, and thus made it possible for them to mix with the rest of mankind, and hold intercourse with their neighbours. Next he built a church for them in a place called Schamalinichon, in order that they might perform divine service, partake of the holy mysteries, gain the favour of God by prayers, perform the other duties of religion, and feel themselves to be human beings. He built forts in every part of the country, garrisoned them with regular Roman soldiers, and thus enabled the Tzani to mix without restraint with the rest of mankind. I shall now describe the parts of Tzania in which he built these forts.

There is there a place where the three frontiers of the Roman Empire, of Persian Armenia, and of the Tzani join; here he constructed a new and very powerful fort, named Oronon, which he made the chief guarantee of peace to the country; for at that point the Romans first entered Tzania. Here he established a garrison under a general with the title of Duke. At a place distant two days' journey from Oronon, on the frontier of the Ocenite Tzani—for the Tzani are divided into many tribes—there was a fortress built in ancient times, which long before this had fallen into ruin by neglect, and was named Charton. The Emperor Justinian restored this, and placed in it a large garrison to keep the province in order.

On the east of this place is a precipitous ravine stretching towards the north. Here he built a new fort named Barchon. Beyond this, at the skirts of the mountain, are stables where the Ocenite Tzani used to keep their cattle, not in order to plough the land,—for the Tzani, as I said before, are altogether idle, and know nothing of husbandry, and have no ploughed land, or other operations of farming,—but for a constant supply of milk and meat. Beyond the skirts of the mountain, to the westward of the place upon the plain, which is called Cena, stands the fort of Sisilisson, which was of ancient construction, but by length of time had fallen into ruin, and was restored by the Emperor Justinian, who established in it, as in all the others, a sufficient garrison of Roman soldiers. On the left, as one goes from thence in a northerly direction, is a place which the natives call the Ditch of Longinus; for in ancient times Longinus, a Roman general of the Isaurian nation, pitched his camp there during a campaign against the Tzani. Here our Emperor built a fort, named Burgum Noes, a day's journey distant from Sisilisson, which, like the fort at Sisilisson described above, our Emperor very strongly fortified. Beyond this is the frontier of the Coxylini Tzani, where he placed two forts named Schimalinichon and Tzanzakon. Here he placed another officer with a garrison.

VII. These were the works of the Emperor Justinian among the Tzani. In the country beyond them, on the banks of the Euxine Sea, is a city called Trapezus.* As there was a scarcity of water at this place, the Emperor Justinian constructed an aqueduct, called by the name of the Martyr Eugenius, by which he relieved the wants of the inhabitants. Both here and at Amasea† he restored

* Trapezus now Trebizond. (W.)

† Amasea (Amasia). 'Hamilton found two Hellenic towers of beautiful construction on the heights. But the greater part of the walls now standing are Byzantine or Turkish. (See " Researches in

the greater part of the churches, which had become ruinous by lapse of time. Beyond the frontier of the city of Trapezus is a place named Rhizeum,* which he in person restored and surrounded with fortifications magnificent beyond description and belief; for the city is second to none of those on the Persian frontier in size and strength.

He also built a fort in Lazica, named Losorium, and fortified the passes in that country, which are named the Clisuræ, in order to shut out the enemy from the country of the Lazi.† He also restored an ancient and ruinous church of the Christian Lazi, and founded a noble city, named Petra,‡ which the Lazi by their own negligence allowed to fall into the hands of the Persians, when Chosroes came thither with a great army; but the Romans conquered the Persians in battle, killed some of them, took the rest prisoners, and razed the city to the ground, that the Persians might not be able to return thither and do any more mischief—all of which has been described in my 'History of the Wars'—where also is a description of how, on the Continent opposite the territory of the Lazi, as one goes towards the Mæotic Lake,§ the Romans destroyed two forts, named Sebastopolis‖ and Pityous, because they heard that Chosroes meditated sending an

---

Assyria," vol. ii., p. 16.) Hamilton explored a passage cut in the rock, about 300 feet, to a small pool of clear cold water.'—Chesney, p. 535. The tombs described by Strabo remain. They are supposed to have been built by Mithridates.

* Rhizeum now Rizeh, to the east of Trebizond. (W.)

† This country was known to the Greeks and Romans as Colchis.

‡ A town of the Lazi or Colchis, founded by a general of Justinian to keep the Lazi in subjection. Taken by Chosroes, 541 ; retaken, 551, by Romans and destroyed. See Procopius, B. Per. and Bel. Got., and Gibbon. Its ruins are now called Oudjenar. (L.)

'The sole vestige of Petra subsists in the writings of Procopius and Agathias.'—Gibbon, ch. xiii. (S.)

§ Sea of Azof. (W.)

‖ Formerly Dioscurias, on eastern shore of Black Sea. (W.)

army to occupy them. Now, however, the Emperor Justinian entirely rebuilt Sebastopolis, which before was only a small fort, making it impregnable by the strength of its walls and other defences, and ornamenting it with streets and buildings, so as to render it one of the first of cities, both for size and beauty.

Moreover, finding that the walls of the cities of Bosporus and Cherson, which are situated upon the sea-shore in that region, beyond the Mæotic Lake and the Tauri and the Tauroscythi, on the frontier of the Roman Empire, had quite fallen into ruin, he restored them to a condition of great beauty and strength. In the same region he built the fort of Alustus, and one in the country of the Gorzubiti. He especially strengthened the fortifications of Bosporus, which, in ancient times, had fallen into the power of the barbarians, and which he captured from the Huns and annexed to the Roman Empire. There is here a country by the sea-shore, named Doru, which has been long inhabited by those Goths, who would not follow Theoderic on his expedition to Italy, but of their own accord remained there, and have been in alliance with the Romans down to my own time, joining the Roman armies when they march against the enemy, at the pleasure of the Emperor; their numbers are about three thousand; they are excellent warriors, industrious husbandmen, and most hospitable to strangers. Their country, Doru, is situated on high ground, yet is not rough or sterile, but good soil, producing the best of crops. The Emperor built no city or fort anywhere in this country, as its inhabitants cannot endure to be confined within walls, but love to dwell in the open country. He did, however, fortify with long walls the passes by which an enemy could enter the country, and thus freed the Goths from foreign invasion. These were his works in this quarter.

There is a maritime town of the Thracians on the

borders of the Euxine Sea, named Anchialus,* which it would be more proper to mention in my description of Thrace; since, however, the course of my narrative has led me to speak of the works of our Emperor on the shores of the Euxine Sea, it will be well at this point to describe the buildings which he erected at Anchialus. At this place, fountains of warm water, which spring up not far from the city, supply the inhabitants with natural baths. This place was neglected and left unfortified by the former Emperors, although so many tribes of barbarians dwell in the neighbourhood of it, so that the sick persons, who resorted to it, could not enjoy its benefits without considerable danger; however, the Emperor Justinian has now fortified it, and enabled them to be healed in safety. These were the fortifications built in the East, in Armenia, in the country of the Tzani, and on the shores of the Euxine Sea, by the Emperor Justinian. Let us now proceed from this region to the buildings which he has constructed in the rest of Europe.

BOOK IV.

I. I COUNT it a toilsome and perilous task, to cross a great ocean in a crazy vessel; and it is the same thing to describe the buildings of the Emperor Justinian in a feeble narrative; for this Emperor, one may say, showed greatness of mind in all that he did, and in his buildings performed works surpassing description. In Europe especially, wishing to construct works on a scale worthy of the need which existed for them, his buildings are difficult, nay, almost impossible to describe, being worthy of their position in the neighbourhood of the river Danube and

* Now Anchialo in Eastern Roumelia. (W.)

the barbarian tribes beyond it, whose invasions they are intended to repel; for along its banks dwell the nations of the Huns and the Goths, and the empire is threatened by the tribes of the Tauri and the Scythians, the Sclavonians and the rest, whom the ancient historians call the 'dwellers in waggons' or Sauromatæ, and all the other wild tribes which either inhabit or roam through that region. With all these tribes, ever eager for war, Justinian was forced to contend, so that he could neglect no point, but was forced to construct a chain of innumerable fortresses, establish in them numberless garrisons of soldiers, and do everything else in his power to hold in check a foe, with whom neither truce nor intercourse could be held; for these enemies were accustomed to make war without any pretext or declaration, and not to terminate it by any treaty, or cease fighting after a time, but to take up arms without any cause only to lay them down when compelled by main force. However, let us proceed to what remains of our description; for when a work is begun, it is better to bring it to an end in any fashion whatever, rather than to give it up and leave it unfinished; besides which, we might reasonably be blamed if our Emperor could construct such works, and we were to shrink from the labour of describing them. Now that I am about to enumerate the buildings of this our Emperor in Europe, it is worth while before doing so to make a few remarks about the country.

From what is called the Adriatic Sea a branch extends straight into the continent, apart from the rest of the sea, so as to divide the country and form the Ionian Gulf, having on its right bank the Epirotes and the other nations in that quarter, and on the left the Calabrians. Compressed into a long and narrow inlet, it embraces almost the whole of the continent. Above this sea and running over against it, the river Danube forms the land of Europe into a peninsula. Here our Emperor constructed many admirable works; for he fortified the whole of Europe so securely as to render it inaccessible to the barbarians who dwell beyond the river Danube.

I ought, however, to begin with the native country of the Emperor, which must occupy the first place in my narrative, as it does in all other respects; for it alone may rejoice and pride itself upon the glory of having bred and furnished the Romans with an Emperor, whose works are so great that they can neither be described in language nor set down in writing.

In the country of the European Dardani, who dwell beyond the frontier of the citizens of Epidamnus, near the fort called Bederiana, is a place named Tauresium, from whence came the Emperor Justinian, the Founder of the Universe.* This place he hastily fortified in a quadrangular form, placing a tower at each angle, and gave it from its shape the name of Tetrapyrgia, or the 'Four Towers.' Close to this place he built a most noble city, which he named Justiniana Prima (this word in the Latin language means 'First'), thus repaying his debt to the country which bred him, though this duty ought to have been shared by all the Romans, since this place furnished a preserver for them all alike. Here he constructed an aqueduct and supplied the city with a perpetual flow of water, and erected many other works, magnificent and surpassing all description, worthy of the founder of the city; it is not easy to enumerate the churches, and it is

* 'Under the name of Justiniana Prima, the obscure village of Tauresium became the seat of an archbishop and a præfect, whose jurisdiction extended over seven warlike provinces of Illyricum; and the corrupt appellation of *Giustendil* still indicates, about twenty miles south of Sophia, the residence of a Turkish sanjak.'—Gibbon, ch. xl. (S.)

impossible for language to describe the dwellings of the magistrates, the size of the porticos, the beauty of the market-places, the fountains, the streets, the baths, and the shops. In a word, the city is great, populous, flourishing, and worthy to be the metropolis of the whole country, to which dignity it has been raised. In addition to this, it is the seat of the Archbishop of Illyria, all the other cities yielding to it as being the greatest in size; so that it in turn reflects glory upon the Emperor; for the city prides itself upon the Emperor which it has bred, while the Emperor glories in having constructed the city. Let the above description of it suffice; for to describe it all, in exact detail, is impossible, because all language must fall short of a city worthy of such an Emperor.

Besides this, he entirely rebuilt the fort of Bederiana, and rendered it much stronger than before. There was an ancient city in the country of the Dardani, named Ulpiana. He demolished the greater part of the wall of this place, which was very unsafe and altogether useless, and brought it to its present magnificent appearance, decorated it with many other beautiful buildings, and gave it the name of Justiniana Secunda. (Secunda in the Latin language signifies 'Second.') He also built a new city in its neighbourhood, which he named Justinopolis, after the name of his uncle Justin. He restored the walls of Sardica, Naïsopolis, Germana and Pantalia, which he found dilapidated by age, so as to make them secure and impregnable. Between these cities he built three small towns, Cratiscara, Quimedaba, and Rumisiana. Thus he restored these cities from their foundations; and, wishing to render the river Danube a very strong bulwark to them and to the whole cf Europe, he covered the whole course of the river with numerous forts, as I shall shortly afterwards describe, and established on all parts of its banks garrisons of soldiers, sufficient to restrain the barbarians from crossing the river in that quarter. When, however, he had completed all these works, remembering the insecurity of all human designs, and reflecting that, should the enemy succeed in passing the river by any means, they would ravage the unguarded country, carry off all the inhabitants for slaves, and plunder all their property, he did not leave them to trust to the forts along the course of the river alone for their protection, but gave them means of defence of their own; for he constructed such a number of fortifications in these regions, that every field either possesses a castle or is near to some walled place, both here and in New and Old Epirus. Here also he built the city of Justinianopolis, which formerly was called Adrianopolis.

He restored Nicopolis, Photica and Phœnice; the latter towns, Photica and Phœnice, being situated upon low ground, suffered from inundations; wherefore the Emperor Justinian, perceiving that it was impossible to build walls for them upon a firm foundation, made no alteration in either of them, but built forts near them, which he placed upon strong and precipitous ground. In this country there was an ancient city, abundantly supplied with water, and deriving its name from its position, for it was formerly named Eurœa. Not far from this city of Eurœa is a lake, in the midst of which rises an island containing a hill; the lake reaches round this island so far as only just to allow access to it. The Emperor transferred the inhabitants of Eurœa to this place, built a city for them, and strongly fortified it.

II. After our survey of the whole of Epirus we pass over Ætolia and Acarnania, and come to the Crissæan Gulf, the Isthmus of Corinth, and the other parts of Greece. Here the Emperor's foresight was most especially displayed, and one may marvel at the numerous walled cities with which he fortified the Roman Empire. Amongst the rest he paid especial care at the pass of Thermopylæ. In the first place he raised its walls to a great height, for the mountains in this place were easy to be taken by an enemy, and were fortified by what was more like a hedgerow than a wall. He placed double battlements upon all these walls, and also upon the fort, which had been built there in an equally careless manner by the ancients, giving it a sufficient height, and double bulwarks. Besides all this, as the place was entirely without water, he contrived a reservoir for rain-water, and also carefully fortified many paths up the mountain which had formerly been left unguarded.

One may well wonder how the Persian King spent so long a time here, and only found one path, and that, too, one which was betrayed to him by Greek traitors, when there are many unfortified roads in the place along which one could almost drive a waggon; for the sea, which washes the base of the mountains, has widened the mouths of most of the paths leading up from thence, and as the ground was full of glens and impassable ravines, it appeared to the ancients that what was thus divided by nature could not be continuously enclosed by fortifications, so that they lazily sacrificed their safety in their reluctance to embark upon so difficult a work, and trusted to chance, resting all their hopes of safety against the invasion of the barbarians on their probable ignorance of the roads; for men who despair of accomplishing difficult tasks always imagine that what they have found so hard, will not easily be effected by others; so that it cannot be disputed that the Emperor Justinian showed greater care and foresight than anyone else who has ever lived, since he was not prevented, even by the sea which washes and breaks upon these mountains, from laying firm foundations on the very beach and watery shore, and making the most contrary elements serve his purpose, and yield to him, subdued by human art. However, not even after having connected these mountain thickets and glens, and having joined the sea to the mountain, and enclosed the whole of Greece with his fortifications, did our Emperor relax his zeal on behalf of his subjects, but he also built many forts within this wall, taking a just view of the chances of human life, which render no place secure or impregnable; so that if by any mischance it should happen that these walls should at any time be taken, the garrison might find a refuge in these forts. Moreover, he established everywhere granaries and reservoirs of water in secure positions, and placed nearly 2,000 soldiers to garrison the works, which was never done by any emperor at any former time; for these walls remained unguarded formerly, even down to my own time, and if the enemy assaulted them, some of the peasants in the neighbourhood, adopting a military life on the spur of the moment, used to act as garrison, and, from their want of experience, risked the capture of them and of the whole of Greece, by which parsimony this country was for a long time exposed to the attack of the barbarians.*

Thus did the Emperor Justinian strengthen the fortifications of Thermopylæ. He also with great care built walls round the cities which lie in the country beyond it—

---

* 'From the edge of the seashore, through the forests and valleys, and as far as the summit of the Thessalian Mountains, a strong wall was continued, which occupied every practical entrance. Instead of a hasty crowd of peasants, a garrison of 2,000 soldiers was stationed along the rampart; granaries of corn and reservoirs of water were provided for their use; and by a precaution that inspired the cowardice which it foresaw, convenient fortresses were erected for their retreat.'—Gibbon, ch. xl. (S.)

Saccus, Hypata, Coracii, Unnum, Baleæ and Leontarium. At Heraclea he did as follows: as one goes from Illyria to Greece, two mountains stand close to one another for a long distance, forming a narrow pass between them, of the kind called Clisuræ. In the midst runs a fountain, which in the summer-time pours a clear and drinkable stream down from the mountains which stand around, and forms a tiny rivulet; but in rainy seasons there rises a very deep and violent torrent, which collects its waters from the ravines among the cliffs. By this path the barbarians were able to gain an easy passage to Thermopylæ and the neighbouring parts of Greece. On either side of the path there were in ancient times two ancient fortresses, one being the city of Heraclea, which I mentioned before, and the other that of Myropole, standing at a little distance from it. The Emperor Justinian restored both these fortresses, which had long been in ruins, and built a very strong wall across the pass, joining it to the mountains on either side, so that he closed the passage against the barbarians, and forced the torrent first to form a lake within this wall, and then to flow over it and continue its course.

He secured all the cities of Greece which lie within the walls of Thermopylæ, restoring the fortifications of all of them, for they had long ago fallen into decay—at Corinth in consequence of violent earthquakes, and at Athens, Platæa, and the towns in Bœotia having fallen into decay through age, as no one had taken any care of them; he, however, left no place assailable or unguarded, for in his watchful care for his subjects he bethought him that the barbarians, should they reach the country about Thermopylæ, would despair of success as soon as they learned that they would gain nothing by forcing the works there, since all the rest of Greece was fortified, and they would have to undertake the siege of each individual city; for a deferred hope does not encourage men to endure labour, nor are they eager for gain which is far distant, but give up their hopes of future advantage to avoid present discomfort.

Having effected this, the Emperor Justinian, learning that all the cities in Peloponnesus were unwalled, and reflecting that much time would be wasted if he attended to the security of each one, securely fortified the whole isthmus with a wall, since the existing wall was mostly in ruins. Upon this wall he built forts and established garrisons in them, and in this manner rendered the whole country of Peloponnesus safe from the enemy, even though any misfortune should befall the fortifications at Thermopylæ.

III. Diocletianopolis in Thessaly was in ancient times a flourishing city, but latterly was ruined by the incursions of the barbarians, and had long been without inhabitants. There is a lake near it, which is called Castoria, in the midst of which is an island surrounded by water, with only one narrow passage, not wider than fifteen feet, leading to it through the lake. On this island stands a very lofty mountain, which overhangs the lake on one side and the island on the other; wherefore our Emperor decided against the site of Diocletianopolis, because it was obviously exposed to attack, and had long before suffered the misfortunes which I had mentioned, but built a very strong city on the island, to which he naturally gave his own name. Besides this, he removed the walls of Echinæum, Thebes, Pharsalus, and all the other cities of Thessaly, amongst which are Demetrias, Metropolis, Gomphi, and Tricattus, and securely fortified them, for their walls were decayed by age and could easily be taken by an enemy.

Now that we have come to Thessaly, let us proceed to

Mount Pelion and the river Peneus. The Peneus flows in a gentle stream past Mount Pelion, and in its course adorns the city of Larissa, for Phthia no longer exists, but has perished through age. The river flows with a quiet stream as far as the sea, and the neighbouring country is rich in fruits of all kinds, and in sweet waters, which the inhabitants were never able to enjoy, as they were in continual expectation of an attack from the barbarians; for there was no strong place anywhere in these regions to which they could fly for refuge, but the walls of Larissa and Cæsarea were so ruinous that they were almost open towns. The Emperor Justinian, by rebuilding the walls of both these cities very strongly, enabled the country to enjoy true prosperity. Not far from hence rise precipitous mountains covered with lofty trees. These mountains were the home of the Centaurs; and in this country the battle of the Centaurs with the Lapithæ took place, as the ancient myths declare, which inform us that in old times there dwelt there a monstrous race combining the forms of two creatures. Antiquity gives some warrant for this fable by the name of a fort in these mountains, which down to my own time was named Centauropolis, whose ruinous walls the Emperor Justinian restored and strengthened, together with those of Eurymene in the same country, which had fallen into the same condition.

Now, that I may leave no part of Greece undescribed, we must proceed to the island of Eubœa, which stands close to Athens and Marathon. This island of Eubœa lies in the sea, in front of Greece, and seems to me as though it had once formed a part of the mainland, and had afterwards been separated from it by a strait, for an arm of the sea flows past the mainland there, in the neighbourhood of the city of Chalcis, ebbing and flowing in a narrow channel, confined between banks which reduce it to the size of a rivulet. This strait is called the Euripus. Such is the island of Euboea. A single beam laid across the strait forms a bridge, which the inhabitants lay across at their pleasure, and then appear to be dwellers on the continent, and walk on foot to the land beyond the strait; but when they remove it, they cross the strait in boats, and again become islanders: so that whether they proceed on foot or on shipboard depends upon the laying down or taking up of a single piece of wood. . . .

The country within this is named (the Peninsula of) Pallene. In ancient times the inhabitants built a wall across the isthmus, which joined the sea at each end, and built there a city, which in former times was called Potidæa, and now Casandria; however, time so ruined all these buildings that when, not long ago, the Huns overran these regions, they captured this cross-wall and city as though in sport, though they never have conducted a siege since the world began. This event, however, gave the Emperor Justinian an opportunity of displaying his goodness and magnanimity: for as he was always wont to repair all the misfortunes which befell him by his own foresight, he turned the most terrible disasters into a source of good fortune by the magnificent works by which he repaired. So here he fortified the city of Pallene, which is the bulwark of the whole country, and the wall across the isthmus, so as to render them quite impregnable and able to defy all attacks. These were his works in Macedonia.

Not far from the city of Thessalonica flows the river Rhechius, which passes through a fertile and rich country, and empties itself into the sea at that place. This river flows with a gentle current: its waters are calm and sweet. The neighbouring country is low-lying, well-watered, and forms rich pasture; but was sadly exposed to the inroads of the barbarians, having no fort or place of strength of any kind for a distance of forty miles; wherefore the Emperor built a strong fort on the banks of the river Rhechius where it joins the sea—an entirely new work, to which he gave the name of Artemisium.

IV. It is my duty to mention the other strong places in this part of Europe. I am quite sure that if I were to recount this list of the fortresses in this country, to men dwelling in a distant region and belonging to another nation, without any facts to guarantee the truth of my story, the number of the works would make it appear altogether fabulous and incredible; as it is, however, they are to be seen at no great distance, and great numbers of the inhabitants of that region are present in our city; wherefore, with the confidence which springs from truth, I shall not hesitate to give a list of the works of the Emperor Justinian in the above-mentioned countries, both in restoring ruinous fortifications and in building new ones. It will be most convenient to put them all in the form of a list, so that my narrative may not be confused by the insertion of their names.

These are the new forts built by the Emperor Justinian in New Epirus :*

Sceminites,	Martis,
Ulpiansus,	Gynæcomytes,
Episterba,	Speretium,
Argus,	Aven,
Aona,	Streden,
Stephaniacum,	Deuphracus,

* 'Six hundred of these forts were built or repaired by the Emperor; but it seems reasonable to believe, that the far greater part of them consisted only of a brick or stone tower, in the midst of a square or circular area, which was surrounded by a wall and ditch, and afforded in a moment of danger some protection to the peasants and cattle of its neighbouring villages.'—Gibbon, ch. xl. (S.)

St. Sabinus,	Labellus,
Aliula,	Epileum,
Dyrlachin,	Piscinæ,
Patana,	Cithinas,
Gemenus,	Dolebin,
Bacuste,	Hedonia,
Alistrus,	Titiana,
Irene,	Ulibula,
Epiduta,	Brebate,
Bacusta,	Thesaurus.

These places were restored:

St. Stephen,	Tithra,
Cethreon,	Brebeta,
Apis,	Bupus,
Peleum,	Endyni,
Come,	Dionysus,
Pacue,	Ptochium,
Scidreonpolis,	Tyrcanus,
Antipagræ,	Capaza,
Pupsalus,	Cilicæ,
Gabræum,	Argyas,
Dionaa,	Therma,
Clementiana,	Amantia,
Illyrin,	Paretium.

These are the new forts built in Old Epirus:

Parmus,	Xeropotoes,
Olbus,	Europa,
Cionin,	Chimæra,
Marciana,	Helega,
Algus,	Homonœa,
Cimenus,	Adanum.

These places were rebuilt:

- Murciara,
- Castina,
- Genysius,
- Percus,
- Marmarata,
- Listria,
- Petroniana,
- Carmina,
- St. Sabinus,
- Also a reservoir in the fort of Come,
- Martius,
- Pezium,
- Onalus,
- Two forts dedicated to St. Donatus, in the territory of Justinianopolis and Photice,
- Symphygium,
- Pronathidum,
- Hedones,
- Castellum,
- Bulibas,
- Palyrus,
- Trana,
- Posidon,
- Colophonia.

In Macedonia:

- Candida,
- Colobona,
- The Basilica of Amyntas,
- Bolbus,
- Brigizes,
- Opas,
- Pleurum,
- Caminus,
- Therma,
- Bogas,
- Neapolis,
- Calarnus,
- Museum,
- Acremba,
- Adrianium,
- Edana,
- Melichisa,
- Pascas,
- Aulon,
- Gentianum,
- Priniana,
- Thesteum,
- Cyrrhi,
- Gurasson,
- Cumarciana,
- Limnederium,
- Bupoodin,
- Babas,
- Cyriana,
- Pelecum,
- Lages,
- Cratæa,

Siclæ,
Nymphium,
Metizus,
Argicianum,
Bazinus,
Cassopas,
Parthion,

Fasciæ,
Placidiana,
Hynea,
Limnaæ,
Option,
Charadrus,
Cassopes.

These forts were rebuilt in Thessaly:

Alcon,
Lossonus,
Gerontica,
Perbyla,

Cercinei,
Scidreus,
Phracellan.

The following new forts were built in Dardania:

Laberium,
Castimum,
Rabestum,
Castellium,

Acrenza,
Terias,
Drullus,
Victoriæ.

These were rebuilt:

Cesiana,
Tezule,
Usiana,
Besiana,
Mascas,
Liste,
Celliriana,
Zysbaës,
Genzana,
Petrizen,
Eutychiana,
Mulato,

Priscopera,
Miletes,
Dardapara,
Cesuna,
Veriniana,
Lasbarus,
Castellobretara,
Edetzio,
Dinius,
Cecola,
Emastus,
Castelona,

Belas,	Capomalva,
Cattarus,	Seretus,
Cattaricus,	Potchium,
Pentza,	Quino,
Cattapheterus,	Berzana,
Debanus,	Bessaiana,
Cubinus,	Arsa,
Getmaza,	Blezo,
Victoriana,	Labutza,
Azeta,	Quinti,
Durbulie,	Bermerium,
Suricum,	Catrasema,
Cusines,	Rotun,
Tuttiana,	Cobenciles,
Ballesina,	Marcellina,
Bella,	Primoniana,
Catrelates,	Pamylinus,
Casyella,	Aria.
Mariana,	

These in the country of the city of Sardica:

Scupium,	Struas,
Stenes,	Protiana,
Marcipetra,	Maccunniana,
Briparum,	Scopentziana.
Romaniana,	

In the country of Cabentza, Balbæ was built, and the following were repaired:

Byrsia,	Vineus,
Stamazo,	Trisciana,
Clesbestita,	Parnusta,
Duiana,	Tzimes,

Turicla,
Medeca,
Peplabius,
Cunæ,

Bidzo,
Stenocorta,
Danedebæ,
Ardia.

In * * * these were restored:

Bugarma,
Betzas,
Bregedaba,

Borbrega,
Turus.

These were rebuilt:

Salebries,
Arcunes,
Duries,
Buteries,
Barbaries,
Arbatias,
Cuzusura,
Etæries,
Itaberies,
Tugurias,
Bemaste,
Stramentias,

Bottes,
Bitzimaeas,
Badziania,
Banes,
Bimerus,
Tusudeaas,
Scuanes,
Scentudies,
Scares,
Lignius,
Itadeba.

In the country of the city Germanae, Scaplizo was built, and the following were rebuilt:

Germas,
Candaras,
Rolligeras,

Scinzeries,
Riginocastellum,
Suagogmense.

These in the country of the city of Pauta (Pantalia?):

Tarporum,
Sobastas,
Cherdusceras,

Blepus,
Zespuries.

These in the region of Scassetana:

    Alarum,   Balausum,
    Magomias,   Butis.
    Luconanta,

In the country of the city of * * * these new forts were built:

    Calventia,   Arsaza,
    Pharanores,   Viculea,
    Stranbasta,   Castellium,
    Aldanes,   Groffes,
    Barachthestes,   Garces,
    Sarmates,   Pistes,
    Arsena,   Dusmanes,
    Brarcedum,   Bratzista,
    Eraria,   Holodoris,
    Bercadium,   Cassia,
    Sabinibries,   Grandetum,
    Timiana,   Urbriana,
    Candilar,   Nogeto,
    Gurbicum,   Mediana,
    Lautzones,   Tiuncana,
    Duliares,   Castengium.

These were rebuilt:

    Hercula,   Millareca,
    The fort of Mucianus,   Debrera,
    Burdopes,   Chesdupara.
    Calys,

These in the country of Remesiana:

    Brittura,   Cumudeba,
    Subaras,   Deurias,

Lamponiana,
Stronges,
Dalmatas,
Primiana,
Frerraria,
Topera,
Tomes,
Cuas,
Tzerzenuzas.
Stenes,
Aeadaba,
Deutreba,
Pretzuries,

Lutzolo,
Repordenes,
Spelunca,
Scumbro,
Britaro,
Tulcoburgo,
Longiana,
Lupofantana,
Dardapara,
Burdomina,
Grinciapana,
Graccus,
Drasimarca.

In the country of Aquiena there was built the new fort of Timathachion, and the following were rebuilt:

Peteres,
Sculcoburgo,
Vindimiola,
Braiola,
Arganocilum,
Auriliana,
Gembro,
Clemades,
Turribas,
Gribo,
Chalarus,
Tzutrato,
Mutzipara,
Stendas,
Scaripara,
Odriuzo,
Cipipene,
Trasiana,

Castellonovo,
Florentiana,
Romyliana,
Sceptecasas,
Argentares,
Potes,
Amuloselotes,
Timalciolum,
Meridio,
Meriopontede,
Tredetitilius,
Bræola,
Motrees,
Vicanovo,
Quartiana,
Julioballæ,
Pontzas,
Zanes.

V. Thus did the Emperor Justinian fortify the whole Illyrian continent. I shall now set forth the manner in which he strengthened the bank of the river Ister, which men also call the Danube, with fortifications and garrisons of soldiers. The Roman Emperors in ancient times, wishing to prevent the barbarians who dwelt beyond the Danube from crossing it, occupied the whole shore of this river with fortresses, which they built not only on the right bank, but in some places also on the further bank of the river. These fortresses were not constructed so as to be inaccessible to assailants, but just sufficient not to leave that bank of the river without defenders; for the barbarians in that region did not understand siege operations. Most of these strong places consisted only of one tower, and were consequently called towers, and very few men were stationed in them. This was at that time sufficient to overawe the barbarian tribes, so that they made no attacks upon the Romans; but in later times Attila invaded the country with a great army, razed all these fortresses to the ground without difficulty, and laid waste the greater part of the Roman territory, without meeting with any resistance. The Emperor Justinian rebuilt the demolished forts, not in their original form, but in the most powerful manner of fortification, and in addition to them built many others. In this manner he entirely restored the security of the Roman Empire, which had been altogether lost. I shall now set forth the manner in which all this was effected.

The river Danube, flowing from the mountains of the Celts, who are now known as the Gauls, encloses a great tract of country, for the most part entirely desert, but in some places inhabited by barbarians, who dwell like savages, without any intercourse with the rest of mankind. On reaching Dacia, it first begins to divide the barbarians who dwell on its left bank from the Roman territory on the right bank. For this reason the Romans call this part of Dacia 'Ripensis'; for in the Latin language a bank is called *ripa*. The first city which they built on this bank was named Singedon, which in process of time the barbarians captured, razed to the ground, and rendered entirely desolate. Most of the other fortresses were reduced to the same condition; but the Emperor Justinian rebuilt it entirely, surrounded it with a strong wall, and again made it a noble and admirable city. He built a new fort of great strength, distant eight miles from the city of Singedon,* which from that circumstance is called Octavum. Beyond it there was an ancient city named Viminacium, which the Emperor entirely rebuilt; for it had long before been razed to the ground.

VI. Proceeding onward from the city of Viminacium, three fortresses stand on the bank of the Danube, named Picnus, Cupus, and Novæ, which formerly derived their name from a single tower built in each place; now, however, the Emperor Justinian added so many houses and fortifications to each of these, that they came to be regarded as considerable cities. On the further bank, opposite Novæ, stood in ancient times a ruinous tower named Litorata, which the ancients called Lederata. This place was made by our Emperor into a large and very strong fort. After Novæ are the forts of Cantabazates, Smornes, Campses, Tanatas, Vernes, and Ducepratum, and many more on the further bank, all of which he rebuilt from the foundations. After this comes Caput-bovis, the work of the Roman Emperor Trajan, and beyond it an ancient fort named Zanes, all of which he enclosed with strong fortifications, and rendered them impregnable bulwarks of the empire. Not far from Zanes is a fort named Pontes, where a stream leaves the river, encloses a small portion

* Singidonum, now Belgrade. (W.)

of the bank, and then rejoining its true channel, unites itself to the main river. It does this not by nature, but compelled by human art. I will now describe why it was that the place was named Pontes, and that the Danube was forced to flow round this place.

The Roman Emperor Trajan, a spirited and energetic man, appears to have been irritated at the thought that the boundary of his empire was fixed by the river Danube.* He was anxious, therefore, to throw a bridge across it, in order that he might pass it without its offering any obstacle when he marched against the barbarians beyond it. How he built this bridge I shall take no pains to describe, but shall let that be told by Apollodorus of Damascus, the chief architect of the entire work. No advantage accrued from it to the Romans, and the bridge subsequently was destroyed by the stream of the Danube and by age. Trajan built two forts on either bank of the river, and called that on the further side Theodora and that on the Dacian bank Pontem, from the name of the bridge; for the Romans call a bridge *pons* in Latin. Since after this the river became impassable for ships at this place, owing to the ruins and foundations of the bridge, they forced the river to adopt a new channel and perform a circuit in order to afford them a passage beyond it. Both these forts fell into ruins through age and the assaults of the barbarians; but the Emperor Justinian rebuilt the fort Pontem, on the right bank of the river, with new and powerful fortifications, and thus secured Illyria. As for that on the opposite bank, named Theodora, he thought

* 'Strabo speaks of the "Iron Gate" as the place where the Danube ends and the Ister begins. Trajan's bridge, of twenty or twenty-two stone piers with wooden arches, was built; A.D. 103, just below the rapids of the "Iron Gate," which grind to powder the ice-blocks of winter, and save the piers from the shock which might otherwise destroy them.'—Murray's 'Handbook of Southern Germany.' (S.)

it unnecessary to bestow any care upon it, since it was exposed to the attacks of the barbarians in that region; but he built all the new fortifications which stand on the bank below Pontem at this day, which are named Mareburgus, Susiana, Armata, Timena, Theodoropolis, Stiliburgus, and Halicaniburgus. There is a small city near this place, named Ad Aquas, some small part of whose fortifications, which had become unsafe, were restored by the Emperor. Beyond it he built Bergonovore, and Laccobergus, and the fort named Dorticum, which he made into the existing strong fortification. He altered the solitary tower named Judæus into what may be called, and really is, a most beautiful fort. He rebuilt Bergus Altus, which formerly was deserted and altogether uninhabited, and also enclosed with a wall another place named Gombes. He rebuilt the fortifications of Crispas, which had become ruinous from age, and built Longiniana and Ponteserium in an admirable manner. At Bononia and Novum he rebuilt the bastions which had become ruinous. He rebuilt all the ruinous parts of the city of Ratiaria; and in many other places he either enlarged small fortifications or reduced over-large ones to a convenient form, in order that neither their smallness nor their excessive size might expose them to the attacks of the enemy; as, for example, he turned Mocatiana from a single tower into the more complete fort which it is at this day, whilst at Almus he reduced the space enclosed by the walls, which formerly was very great, thus enabling it to defy the attacks of the enemy. In many places he altered a solitary tower, an object of contempt to an invader, into a strong fort, as at Tricesa and Putedis. He magnificently restored the ruinous walls of Cebrus. He built a new fort in Bigrane, and another one near to it, in a place where formerly stood a single tower named Onos. Not far from this there remained only the foundations of a city, which in former times had been named Augusta, but which now, possessing its ancient name, but having been altogether rebuilt by the Emperor Justinian, is well peopled. He rebuilt the ruined fortifications of Aëdabe, restored the city of Variana, which had long been in ruins, and fortified Valeriana, which before had possessed no defences.

Besides these, he paid attention to and enclosed with strong fortifications other places not on the bank of the river, but standing at a distance from it, named Castramartis, Zetnocortum, and Iscum. He took great pains to enclose with a wall and otherwise fortify an old fort on the bank of the river, named the Fort of the Huns. Not far from the Fort of the Huns is a place where a fort stands on each bank of the Danube, the one in Illyria named Palatiolum, while that on the opposite bank was named Sicibida. These, which had become ruinous through age, were restored by the Emperor Justinian, who thereby checked the inroads of the barbarians in that quarter, and beyond them rebuilt an ancient fort, now known as Utos. On the extreme frontier of Illyria he built a fort named Lapidaria, and altered a solitary tower, named Lucernariaburgum, into a fort worthy of admiration. The above were the works of the Emperor Justinian in Illyria; he did not, however, merely strengthen this country with fortifications, but placed in each of them garrisons of regular soldiers, and thus checked the incursions of the barbarians.

VII. Hitherto I have described the fortifications of Illyria along the river Danube. We must now pass into those which the Emperor Justinian built along its shores in Thrace; for it appears convenient to me first to describe the whole of this bank, and then to proceed to the description of his works in the inland country. Let us then first proceed to the country of the Mysians,* whom the poets speak of as fighting hand to hand; for their country is conterminous with that of Illyria. After Lucernariaburgum, the Emperor Justinian built the new fort of Securisca, and beyond it restored the ruinous part of Cyntodemus. Beyond this he built an entirely new city, which, after the name of the Empress, he called Theodoropolis. He renewed the ruinous part of the forts which are named Iatron and Tigas, and added a tower to that of Maxentius, of which he thought it stood in need. He built the new fort of Cynton. Beyond this is the fortification of Transmarisca, opposite to which, on the further side of the river, the Roman Emperor Constantine once built with great care a fort named Daphne, thinking it advisable that at this place the river should be guarded on both sides. This in process of time was entirely destroyed by the barbarians, but was rebuilt from its foundations by the Emperor Justinian. Beyond Transmarisca, he took suitable pains to restore the fortresses of Altinum and that called Candidiana, which long ago had been destroyed by the same enemies. There are three forts in succession along the bank of the Danube, named Saltopyrgus, Dorostolus, and Sycidaba, in each of which the Emperor repaired with great care such parts as had become ruinous. He bestowed similar pains upon Quesoris, which lies beyond the bank of the river, and enlarged and greatly extended Palmatis, which stands in a narrow pass, although it was not near the bank of the river. Close to this he built a new fort, named Adina, because the Sclavonian barbarians were wont to conceal themselves there and lie in ambush, so as to render it

* Procopius here confounds the Mœsians of Europe with the Mysians of Asia Minor. The passage alluded to is in Homer's 'Iliad,' ii. 604. (S.)

impossible for travellers to proceed through that country. He also built the fort of Tilicion and the outwork on the left of it.

Thus was the bank of the Danube and its neighbourhood fortified in Mysia.* I shall now proceed to Scythia, where the first fort is that named after St. Cyrillus, the ruinous parts of which were most carefully rebuilt by the Emperor Justinian. Beyond this was an ancient fortress named Ulmiton, but as the Sclavonian barbarians had for a long time infested that region, and made their habitation there, it had become quite deserted, and nothing remained of it except its name. He therefore rebuilt it from its foundations, and rendered that part of the country safe from the attacks of the Sclavonians. Next to this is the city of Ibida, whose walls had become very ruinous, but which he, without any delay, rebuilt and rendered very strong. He built a new fort beyond it named Ægistum, and restored another fort in the furthest part of Scythia named Almyris, whose walls had for the greater part fallen into decay, as he did to all the other fortifications in this part of Europe.

VIII. I have described above the buildings constructed by the Emperor Justinian among the Dardanians, Epirotes, Macedonians, and the other tribes of the Illyrians, as well as those in Greece and along the river Ister.

Let us now proceed to Thrace, taking as the best foundation for our narrative the neighbourhood of Byzantium, since that city surpasses all others in Thrace, both in strength and situation, for it overhangs Europe like a citadel, and guards also the sea which divides it from Asia. I have described above his works, both churches and other buildings, within and without the walls of Constantinople; I am now about to speak of what lies beyond them.

* Mœsia.

There is a fort in the suburbs of the city, which from its form is called the 'round fort.' The road which leads from it to Rhegium passes for the most part over uneven ground, and in rainy seasons used to become swampy and difficult for travellers; now, however, our Emperor has paved it with large stones, and made it easy to traverse. In length this road reaches as far as Rhegium; its width is such that two waggons going in opposite directions can pass without difficulty. The stones of which it is formed are very hard; one would imagine them to be millstones. They are of enormous size, so that each of them covers a large extent of ground, and stands up to a great height. They form so smooth and level a surface that they do not seem to be joined, or carefully let into one another, but to have grown together. Such is this road. There is a lake close to Rhegium, into which rivers flowing from the higher ground discharge their waters. This lake reaches as far as the sea, so that there is but one very narrow bank between them, both washed on either side by their several waters; when, however, they approach most nearly to one another, they restrain their currents and turn them back, as though they had there placed boundaries for themselves. At one point they join one another, leaving a channel between them, of which it is hard to say to which water it belongs, for the water of the sea does not always flow into the lake, nor does the lake always discharge its waters into the sea; but after much rain, and with a southerly wind, the water of the channel appears to flow out of the lake; though if the wind blows from the north, the sea appears to wash into the lake. In this place the sea forms an immense extent of shoal-water, with only one narrow channel leading through them into deep water. This channel is so narrow that it is called the 'Ant.' The channel which, as I have said before, joins the lake to the sea, used in former times to be crossed by a wooden bridge, though with great danger to the passengers, who often fell into the water together with the beams of the bridge; now, however, the Emperor Justinian has raised the bridge upon high arches of stone, and rendered the passage safe.

Beyond Rhegium there is a city named Athyra, whose inhabitants he relieved from the distress from which he found them suffering from want of water, by building a reservoir there, in which the excess of their water might be stored up, and supplied to them in time of need; he also restored the ruinous part of their wall.

Beyond Athyra there is a place which the natives call Episcopia. The Emperor Justinian perceiving that this place lay exposed to the attacks of the enemy, more especially as there was no strong place, but the country was entirely unguarded, built a fort there, the towers of which he constructed, not in the usual manner, but as follows. From the 'curtain' wall projects a building, narrow at first, but very wide at the outer end, upon which each of the towers is built. It is not possible for an enemy to approach near to this wall, since they come between these towers, and are overwhelmed by the cross-fire which the garrison easily pour upon their heads. He placed the gates, not in the usual manner, between two towers, but obliquely in a small projection of the wall, so that they are not seen by the enemy, but are hidden behind the wall. This work was performed for the Emperor by Theodorus Silentiarius, a very clever man. Thus was this fort constructed. We must now proceed to make some mention of the 'long walls.'

IX. The sea which proceeds from the ocean and Spain, with Europe on its left hand, flows in the same easterly direction as far as Thrace, but there divides into two portions, one of which proceeds towards the east, while another makes a short bend and terminates in the Euxine Sea. When it reaches Byzantium, it winds round the city on its eastern side, as though round a goal, and continues its course in a much more oblique direction, proceeding by a strait which turns the upper and lower parts of Thrace into an isthmus; not that the sea there is divided into two parts, as is the case in other isthmuses, but it circles round in a singular manner and embraces Thrace on both sides, and more especially the whole suburbs of Byzantium. These suburbs the inhabitants have built over and adorned, not merely for their use, but with an arrogant and boundless luxury, and with all the license which is produced by wealth. Here they have stored much furniture, and preserved many works of art. Whenever, therefore, the barbarians suddenly invade the Roman Empire, these places suffer far more damage than the rest, and are in fact utterly ruined. The Emperor Anastasius, wishing to prevent this, built long walls* at a place no less than forty miles from Byzantium, joining the two seas where they were distant two days' journey from one another. Having constructed these works, he supposed that all within them had been made secure; they were, however, the cause of still greater disasters, for it was not possible either to build so enormous a work firmly, or to guard it with proper care; while when the enemy made themselves masters of one part of the long wall, they conquered the remainder of the garrison without difficulty,

* 'The "long wall," as it was emphatically styled, was a work as disgraceful in the object, as it was respectable in the execution. . . . . At the distance of only forty miles from the capital, Anastasius was constrained to establish a last frontier; his long wall of sixty miles, from the Propontis to the Euxine, proclaimed the impotence of his arms; and as the danger became more imminent, new fortifications were added by the indefatigable prudence of Justinian.'—Gibbon, ch. xl. (S.)

assailed the rest of the people unexpectedly, and did more mischief than can easily be described.

Our Emperor, however, having rebuilt the ruinous part of these walls, and strengthened their weak points so as to assist their defenders, devised the following plan also. He stopped up all the passages leading from one tower to another, and arranged one single means of ascent from the ground, within the walls of each, so that the garrison could, if necessary, block up this passage and defy an enemy, even though he had made his way within the wall, since each tower is sufficient within itself for the defence of its garrison. Within these walls he made the most complete provision for safety, both by the buildings which I have mentioned above, and by restoring the most ruinous part of the wall of the city of Selybria.* These were the works of the Emperor Justinian at the 'long walls.'

The well-known city of Heraclea,† our neighbour on the sea-coast, which formerly, under the name of Perinthus, was the first city in Europe, and now is second to Constantinople alone, not long ago was reduced to great straits by want of water; not that the country near it was waterless, or that those who built the city in ancient times had neglected to supply it with water—for Europe abounds with·fountains, and the ancients took care to make aqueducts—but time, as usual, destroyed the fabric of the aqueduct either through contempt for the age of the building, or encouraged to ruin it by the carelessness of the citizens of Heraclea. This led to Heraclea being left almost without inhabitants; while time produced the same effect upon the palace there, which was a very magnificent building. However, the Emperor Justinian did not neglect this city, but in a truly royal manner furnished it with

---

* Selybria, now Silibri, on Sea of Marmora. (W.)
† Heraclea, now Eregli, on Sea of Marmora. (W.)

sweet and transparent waters, and did not allow the palace to lose its ancient reputation, for he restored the whole of it.

A day's journey from Heraclea is a place by the seaside named Rhædestus, conveniently situated for the navigation of the Hellespont, with a good harbour where merchant-ships can moor and discharge their cargoes in quiet water, and when reloaded can again put to sea without difficulty. It is, however, exposed to attacks of barbarians if they should make a sudden incursion into that country, being neither fortified nor placed on difficult ground; for this reason it was neglected by merchants, who disregarded it through fear of this danger. Now, however, the Emperor Justinian has not only rendered the place itself secure, but has also provided for the safety of all those who dwell in the neighbourhood by building a city at Rhædestus, with a strong wall and of very remarkable size, in which, on an invasion of the barbarians, all the people of the neighbourhood can take refuge and save their lives and property.

X. Thus did the Emperor Justinian at Rhædestus;* I now proceed to his works in the Chersonesus. The Chersonesus projects beyond that part of Thrace, for it runs out into the sea and appears as though it proceeded as far as Asia, and was joined on to it. Its shore forms a promontory near the city of Elæus,† thus dividing the sea into two parts, while it itself is separated from the rest of the mainland by the water which runs into a recess forming what is called the Black Gulf; the rest of it almost forms an island, from which shape it derives its name, for it is called Chersonesus because it is only prevented by a narrow isthmus from being altogether an island. Across this isthmus the ancients carelessly built a wall which

* Rhædestus, now Rodosto, on Sea of Marmora. (W.)

† Elæus, near the south-east extremity of the Gallipoli promontory, opposite the plain of Troy. (W.)

could be scaled with ladders, making it as low and narrow as though they thought they were building a dry stone wall round an out-of-the-way garden. In addition to this they built low and mean works, of the kind called moles, projecting into the sea on either side of the isthmus, and thus fortified the space between the wall and the sea, but in such a manner as not to repel invaders but to invite them to make an attack, so contemptible and easily captured was their fortification. Imagining, however, that they had erected an impassable barrier against the enemy, they did not think it necessary to build any strong place within this wall, for there was no fort or any other place of strength in the Chersonesus, though it extends for a distance of nearly three days' journey. Quite lately the enemy invaded Thrace, made an attempt upon the passage by the seashore, frightened away its guards, forced their way in as if in sport, and gained the other side of the wall without any difficulty.

The Emperor Justinian therefore, in his great care for the safety of his subjects, did as follows: First, he utterly destroyed the ancient wall so that no vestige of it was left. He then built a second wall upon the same site, of considerable width and height; above the battlements of this he built a vaulted roof like a portico to shelter the defenders, while a second range of battlements resting upon these vaults doubled the defensive power of this work against an enemy. After this, at each end of the wall, on the very beach of the sea, he built two of the projecting works named moles, reaching a long way into the water, connected with the wall, and equalling it in height. He also cleaned out the ditch outside the wall and excavated it to a great width and depth; moreover, he placed a garrison of soldiers within these long walls sufficient to hold them against all the barbarians who might attack the Chersonesus. After having made this part so strong and secure, he nevertheless built additional fortifications in the interior, so that if, which God forbid, any disaster should befall the 'long wall,' the people of Chersonesus would nevertheless be safe; for he enclosed the city of Aphrodisias, which before had been for the greater part defenceless, with a very strong wall, and supplied with walls and inhabitants the city of Ciberis, building there baths, hospices, numerous houses, and all that is necessary for a magnificent city. He likewise most securely fortified Callipolis,* which had been left without walls by the ancients, through their trust in the 'long wall.' Here he built storehouses for corn and wine sufficient to supply all the wants of the garrison of the Chersonesus.†

Opposite Abydos is an ancient city named Sestos, which also in former times was uncared-for and possessed no defences. It was overhung by a very steep hill, upon which he built a fort which is quite inaccessible, and impossible to be taken by an enemy. Not far from Sestos is Elæus, where a precipitous rock rises from the sea, raising its summit high in the air and forming a natural fortification. Upon this also the Emperor built a fort, which is difficult to pass by and altogether impregnable; moreover, he built a fort at Thescus, on the other side of the 'long wall,' fortifying it with an exceedingly strong wall. Thus did he provide in all quarters for the safety of the inhabitants of the Chersonesus.

XI. Beyond Chersonesus is the city of Ænus,‡ which

* Callipolis, now Gallipoli. The wall was about on the line of the Gallipoli lines so well known during the Crimean War. (W.)

† 'In an age of freedom and valour, the slightest rampart may prevent a surprise; and Procopius appears insensible of the superiority of ancient times, while he praises the solid construction and double parapet of a wall, whose long arms stretched on either side into the sea; but whose strength was deemed insufficient to guard the Chersonesus, if each city, and particularly Gallipoli and Sestus, had not been secured by their peculiar fortifications.'— Gibbon, ch. xl. (S.)

‡ Ænus, now Enos, at the mouth of the Maritza. (W.)

takes its name from that of its founder; for Æneas was, according to tradition, the son of Anchises. The wall of this place was easy of capture from its lowness, since it did not reach to the necessary height, while it lay completely exposed in the neighbourhood of the sea, where it was washed by the waves. However, the Emperor Justinian raised its walls to such a height that not only they could not be taken, but could not even be assaulted; and, by bringing them down to the seashore and strengthening them in every quarter, rendered Ænus altogether impregnable. Thus he provided for the safety of the city; but the country remained exposed to the incursions of the barbarians, because the (mountains of) Rhodope had been from ancient times deficient in fortifications. In the interior was a village named Bellurus, in wealth and population equal to a city, but always exposed to the plundering attacks of barbarians, on account of its being defenceless, as was also a large extent of country round about it: this place our Emperor made into a city, fortified, and rendered worthy of himself; moreover he also restored with great care all the fortifications which were wanting or had become ruinous in the other cities in the Rhodope Mountains. Among these were Trajanopolis and Maximianopolis, whose walls he rebuilt where they were defective. These were his works in this quarter.

In this country Anastasiopolis was already furnished with walls, but, though lying near the sea, had an undefended sea-beach, so that it often happened that the barbarian Huns seized the vessels which lay there helpless, and extended their ravages to the neighbouring islands. The Emperor Justinian enclosed the whole sea-beach with a fortification, and thus provided for the safety both of the ships and of the islanders. He also constructed a very lofty aqueduct leading to the city from the mountains in the neighbourhood. There is in Rhodope an ancient city named Toperus, which is almost surrounded by a river, and lies at the foot of a lofty hill, from which it had not long before been captured by the barbarian Sclavonians; but Justinian raised its wall to so great a height that it rises above this hill as much as it formerly fell short of it. He built a vaulted portico along the wall, so that the garrison could defend the city in safety against besiegers, and formed each of its towers into a strong castle. He also strengthened it by enclosing the part between the river and the city-wall by a cross-wall. These were the works of the Emperor Justinian in this quarter.

I will now describe the other fortifications which he built in the rest of Thrace, and in what is now called Mount Hæmus. First, he carefully built up what was wanting or ruinous at Philippopolis and Plotinopolis, which were very weakly fortified, although they stood in the neighbourhood of many tribes of barbarians. He also established numberless forts throughout the whole of Thrace, by means of which the country, which had formerly been exposed to the inroads of the enemy, was entirely preserved from their ravages; the names of these forts, as far as my memory goes, are as follows.

In Europe:

Lydicæ,   Elaeae.

In Rhodope the following new forts:

Caseera,   Cuscabri,
Theodoropolis,   Cusculus,
Thrasi,   Thracian Bospara,
Thudanelanæ,   Vesiparum,
Mundepa,   Capisturia,

Tharsandala,
Denizus,
Toparum,
Dalatarba,
Bre,
Scemnas,
Carasthyra,
Pinzus,
Tuleus,
Arzon,
Castrazarba,
Zositersum,
Bergisum,
Dingium,
Sacissus,
Cyrtuxura,
Potamocastellum,
Isdicaea,
Emporium,
Taurocephalaeum,
Velaidipara,
Scitaces,
Bepara,
Pusinum,
Hymanparubri,
Scariotasalucra,
Augustas,
Urdaus,
St. Trajanus,
Dertallus,
Solvani,
Vascum,
Zincyra,
Hæmimonti,

Veripara,
Isgipera,
Ozorme,
Vereiaros,
Tamonbari,
Ditch of Gesilas,
Cheroenum,
Probini,
St. Theodorus,
Burdepto,
Rhacule,
St. Julianus,
Tzitaëtus,
Velastyras,
Getrinas,
Bredas,
Verus,
Thocyodis,
Via,
Anagonclias,
Suras,
Anthipari,
Dordas,
Sarmathon,
Clisura,
Hylasianae,
Thrasarichi,
Bæca,
Chrysanthus,
Marcerota,
Zdebrin,
S. Theodorus,
Asgarzus,
Burtudgizi,

Zemarchi,
Cerioparorum,
Casibonorum,
Unci,
Antoninum,
Debre,
Probini,
Carberus,
Esimonti,
Asgizus,
Dalatarba,
Theodoropolis,
Taurocomum,
Nice,
Cavotumba,
Dixas,
Getistraus,
Tzyidon,
Tzonpolegon,
Basibunum,
Anchialus,
Marcianum,
Cyridana,
Beculi.

The following are the other forts in Thrace on the Euxine Sea and river Danube, and also in the interior of the country.

On the river Danube:

Mysias,
Erculente,
Scatrina,
Appiara,
Exentaprista,
Deoniana,
Limo,
Odyssus,
Bidigis,
Arina,
Nicopolis,
Zicideba,
Poliscastellum,
Cistidizus,
Basternas,
Metalla,
Justinianopolis,
Therma,
Gemellomuntes,
Asilba,
Cuscana,
Cuscum,
Fossatum,
Bisdina,
Marcianopolis,
Scythias,
Grapso,
Nono,
Trosmes,
Naisduno,
Rhesidina,
Constantiana,

Veripara,
Spadizus,
Marcerota,
Bodas,
Zisnudeba,
Turules,
Monteregine,
Becis,
Altina,
Maurovalle,

Callatis,
Bassidina,
Beledina,
Abrittus,
Rubusta,
Diniscarta,
Tigra,
Scedeba,
Novas.

In the interior:

Copustorus,
Virginazo,
Tillito,
Ancyriana,
Murideba,
Itzes,
Castellonovo,
Padisara,
Bismapha,
Valentiniana,
Zaldapa,
Axiopa,
Carso,

Gratiana,
Preidis,
Argamo,
Paulimandra,
Tzasclis,
Fair Theodora,
Tomis,
Creas,
Catassi,
Nisconis,
Novejustiniana,
Presidio,
Ergamia.

And others beyond number.

BOOK V.

1. THE works of Justinian in the whole of Europe have been as far as possible described by me in the former portion of this book; we must now proceed to the description of the remainder of his works in Asia. I think that I have described above the fortifications of cities and forts, and the other buildings erected by him in the East, from the Median frontier as far as the city of Palmyra in Phœnicia, on the borders of Lebanon. I shall now speak of his works in the remainder of Asia and Libya, describing both the manner in which he repaired the roads, which were difficult and dangerous, in some places steep and overhung by rocky mountains, in others bordering upon rivers which drowned travellers, and also how he repaired all that was defective in the cities, beginning at the following point.

Before the city of Ephesus* there is some high ground, not formed of earth or capable of producing fruit, but altogether hard and rocky. Here the inhabitants at former times had built a church, dedicated to St. John the Apostle, surnamed the Divine. This Apostle was named the Divine because he has written about God in a manner surpassing the nature of man. This church, which was small and ruinous through age, the Emperor Justinian

* 'Considerable remains of a church were found on the hill at Ayasalouk. This was perhaps St. John's Church, and was in existence when the Council was held in 431. The Greeks have built for themselves a small church over the site of an ancient Greek church, which was possibly the Church of St. John, as that was known to have been built on a hill.'—'Ephesus,' by J. T. Wood, and Society of Biblical Archæology (London, 1878), p. 332 and 'Discoveries,' p. 164.

'St. John's, at Ephesus, has been destroyed to its foundation. It was in the form of a cross, with a dome at the intersection.'—Texier and Pullan, p. 22. (L.)

razed to the ground, and rebuilt of such size and beauty, that, in short, it resembles and in all respects vies with the church dedicated by him to the Apostles in the imperial city, which I have described above.

This was the work of our Emperor in Ephesus. In the island of Tenedos I will presently describe the work which he constructed for the advantage of the imperial city and all seafarers, after making the following prefatory remarks. The sea as far as the Hellespont is contained in a narrow strait; for the two continents there approach nearest to one another, forming the beginning of the strait near Sestos and Abydos. Ships bound for Constantinople consequently anchor when they reach this place, because they are unable to proceed any further unless the wind blows from the south. When, therefore, the fleet of corn-ships sail thither from Alexandria, if it meets with a favourable wind, the merchants in a very short time moor their ships in the harbours of Byzantium, and as soon as they have unloaded them, depart at once, in order that they may all make this voyage for a second or even a third time before the winter, while those of them who choose take in some other merchandise for the return voyage. If, however, the wind blows against them at the Hellespont, both the corn and the ships become injured by delay. Reflecting upon these things, the Emperor Justinian has clearly proved that nothing is impossible for man, even when he has to contend with the greatest difficulties; for he built granaries on the island of Tenedos, which is close to the strait, of a sufficient size to contain the freight of the whole fleet, being in width no less than ninety feet, in length two hundred and eighty, and of great height. After the Emperor had constructed these, when those who were conveying the public supply of corn were declined by contrary winds at this point, they used to unload their cargo into the granary, and, disregarding the northerly and westerly winds and all the other winds which were unfavourable for them, would prepare for another voyage. They therefore at once sailed home, while afterwards, whenever it became convenient to sail from Tenedos to Byzantium, the corn was conveyed from Tenedos thither in other ships by persons appointed to perform this duty.

II. In Bithynia there is a city* named after Helena, the mother of the Emperor Constantine, in which they say that Helena was born, and which in former times was an inconsiderable village. The Emperor Constantine, out of filial duty, gave this place its name and the dignity of a city, but built nothing there on an imperial or magnificent scale; for the place remained in its former condition in respect of its buildings, but merely had the glory of being called a city, and prided itself on being named after Helena, to whom it had given birth. However, the Emperor of our own age, as though wishing to put away the reproach of the founder of the empire, first supplied this city, which he found suffering from want of water, with a magnificent aqueduct, and furnished the inhabitants beyond their expectation with enough water not only to drink, but also to wash in, and to use for all the other luxuries of life, as they were now supplied with water in abundance; in addition to this he built for them a new public bath, and restored another which had fallen into ruins and been neglected through the want of water which I have mentioned, so that it had all fallen to the ground. He also built churches, palaces, porticos, and dwellings for the magistrates, and supplied all the other needs of a flourishing city.

Close by this city flows a river, which the natives from

* Leake, 'Tour in Asia Minor,' p. 10.

its form call Draco (the snake); for it winds in curves on either hand, often proceeding in opposite directions, bending its waters round in a crooked course, and flowing now to the right hand and now to the left; so that travellers coming to the city were obliged to cross it more than twenty times.* Many of them thus perished through the river suddenly rising in flood; besides which, a thick wood and masses of reeds, which encumbered its outfall into the sea, made it a source of trouble to the country; indeed, not very long ago, after much rain, it overflowed its banks and inundated a great part of the country, doing irreparable damage; for it swept away many fields, uprooted vines, olives, and numberless fruit-trees of all kinds, and also the houses which stood outside the walls of the city, besides doing other important damage to the inhabitants. The Emperor Justinian, out of pity for them, devised the following plan: he cleared away the woods, and cut down all the reeds, so as to enable the river to discharge itself freely into the sea, so that it would no longer be forced to overflow its banks. He also cut through the mountains which stand in that country, and made a carriage-road through places which formerly had been rough and precipitous. By this means he rendered it unnecessary for the greater part of the inhabitants to cross the river at all, whilst he threw two bridges of great width across it, so that henceforth they could pass over it without danger.

III. The excellent works which he constructed at Nicæa,† in Bithynia, are worthy of mention. In the first

---

* See Leake's 'Tour in Asia Minor,' p. 10.

† See Leake's 'Tour in Asia Minor,' pp. 8, 10. (S.)

At the south end of the lake (Arcania), beautifully situated, stood the ruined towers of the famous Nicæa. 'Seldom have I had a harder day's work than in attempting to see and comprehend this ruin of ruins.'

place, he restored the whole of the aqueduct, which had entirely fallen into ruin and become useless, and thus furnished the city with an abundant supply of water. Next he built churches and convents both for women and men. He carefully restored the whole of the palace there, some part of which was in ruins, and likewise a bath in the place which is called the 'Couriers' Lodgings,' and which had long been ruinous. Close to this city, on the west side, a torrent is wont to rush down, making the road in that direction entirely impassable. The ancients had constructed a bridge here, which in the course of time became unable to withstand the rush of the torrent, as it was not kept in proper repair, so that it yielded to the force of the stream, and was swept away, leaving no trace on the spot where it formerly stood. The Emperor Justinian built another bridge here, of such height and width that the former one seemed to bear no proportion to it whatever, which rises high above the torrent when at its fullest, and affords a safe passage to travellers.

At Nicomedia* he rebuilt the Baths of Antoninus, the most important part of which had fallen down, and from the vastness of its size seemed unlikely ever to be rebuilt. The great river which is now called the

---

'The grandeur and peculiar beauty of the arts amongst the earlier Greeks cannot be concealed even in the broken materials.

'Some parts of the walls are entirely Roman; in others the Cross, etc., give the date of the earlier Christians. On three of the towers in the walls of the city are three similar inscriptions. The sign of the Cross is prefixed to all three: "The Tower of Michael, the Great King, Emperor in CHRIST."'—'Travels in Asia Minor,' by Sir C. Fellows (London, 1852), pp. 83, 85.

'A very small church still stands within the present town, which, from its mosaic floor and ceiling, may probably be of the date of St. Mark's at Venice, or rather of the Byzantine age.

'Without the walls is a Roman aqueduct, which still supplies the town with water from the neighbouring mountain.'—Ibid., p. 87. (L.)

* Nicomedia, now Ismid. (W.)

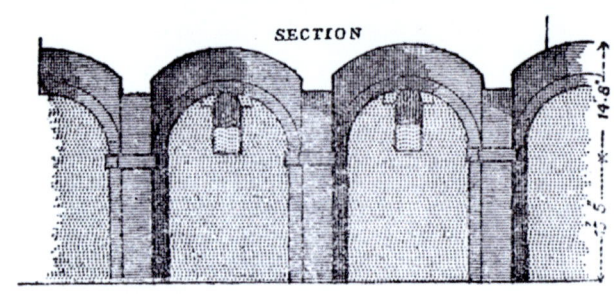

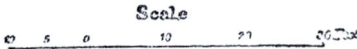

PLAN OF
THE CISTERN OF IMBAHER OR
BATHS OF ANTONINUS.

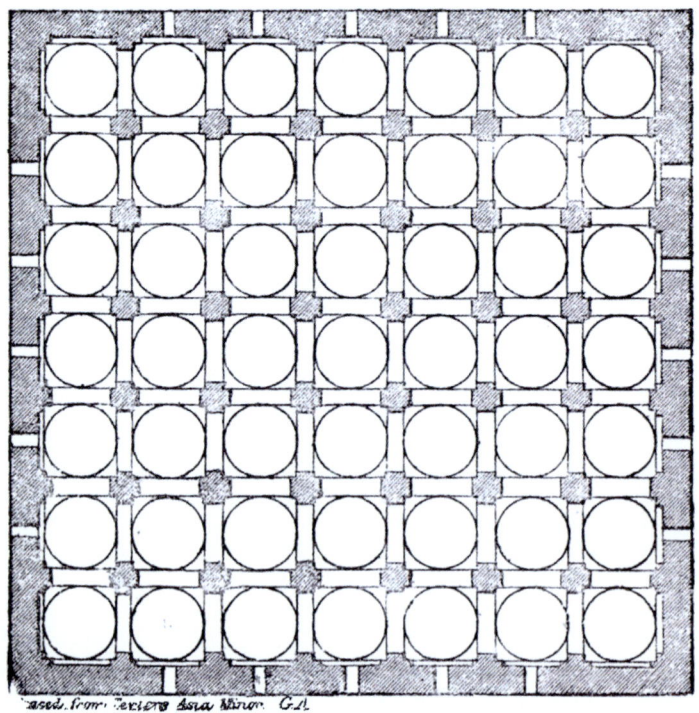

Sangaris,* which runs with an exceedingly swift current, is of great depth in the middle, and of width like a sea, and had never been spanned by a bridge since the creation; however, by lashing a number of boats together, and connecting them with each other like mat-work, foot-passengers ventured to cross it, as once the army of Medes crossed the Hellespont, fearing the wrath of Xerxes. This, however, they did not accomplish without danger, for the river often swept away all the boats, together with their fastenings, and made it impossible for travellers to cross it. Now, however, the Emperor Justinian has attempted to build a bridge over it. The work is begun, and he has already expended much labour upon it; so that I am sure that before long he will accomplish it, for I know that Heaven assists him in all his works, so that up to this time none of his projects have remained unaccomplished, although in many cases he at first seemed to be undertaking impossibilities.

There is a road in Bithynia leading thence into Phrygia, upon which in the winter season innumerable men and animals used to perish; for the ground, being soft, not only after great rains, or the melting of great quantities of snow, but even after slight showers, became deep, impassable mud, and turned the road into a swamp, in which travellers were frequently swallowed up.

* Sangaris, now Sakarieh River. The bridge is now some distance from the river, which has changed its course. (W.)

He, however, together with the Empress Theodora, with magnificent generosity, removed this source of danger to travellers; for they raised the thoroughfare safely upon enormous stones for a distance of half a day's journey for a lightly-equipped traveller, and enabled passengers to proceed along a firm road. These were the works of the Emperor Justinian in this quarter.

In Bithynia there are springs of warm water in the place called Pythia. These springs are made use of by many persons, especially the inhabitants of Byzantium, for pleasure, and above all for the healing of those suffering from disease. Here he displayed a truly imperial magnificence; for he built a palace, which had not existed before, and public baths supplied with the warm water. He also brought hither drinking water by an aqueduct from distant fountains, and relieved the place from the drought from which it had formerly suffered. Besides this, he rebuilt on a larger and much more magnificent scale the Church of the Archangel and the infirmary for the sick.

IV. There is a river in Galatia which the inhabitants call the Siberis,* near the place called Sycæ, and about ten miles from the city of Juliopolis, on the eastern side. This river often rose suddenly to a great height and swept away many of the travellers along that road. The Emperor Justinian, grieved at hearing this, put a stop to these disasters for the future by spanning the river with a powerful bridge, capable of withstanding the force of a flooded river. He also formed the eastern abutment of the bridge into a projecting wall, of the form technically known as a bulwark. He also built a church for travellers on the western side of it, which might serve as a refuge for them in times of storm. The river, which flows past the western side of this city of Juliopolis, used to

---

* Leake's 'Tour in Asia Minor,' pp. 79, 80. (S.)

shake and injure its walls; however, our Emperor restrained it by building an embankment parallel to the city wall for a distance of not less than five hundred feet. By this means he preserved the fortifications of the city from being washed away.

The following were his works in Cappadocia. There has been there since ancient times a very large and populous city named Cæsarea, which was surrounded by a wall of such excessive extent as to render it weak and altogether indefensible, because it enclosed a large space which was not necessary for the city, and was exposed to attack by its useless length; for there are lofty hills, not near to one another, but at a considerable distance, which the founder of the city was anxious to enclose within its walls, lest they should be used to attack it from, so that thus, under the pretext of safety, he really exposed it to great danger, by enclosing many fields and gardens, besides crags and high pasture-land, on which the inhabitants did not subsequently build any houses, but left it in its former condition, the few houses upon it remaining solitary and isolated to the present day. The garrison was not sufficient to guard such a great extent of wall, nor were the inhabitants able to keep it in repair, so that they lived in terror of attack, just as though they had no walls at all. However, the Emperor Justinian pulled down the unnecessary part of the wall, concentrated the city within a really efficient rampart, and made the place impregnable to all assailants, strengthening it with a sufficient garrison. Thus did he provide for the safety of the people of Cæsarea in Cappadocia.

There was in Cappadocia a fortress named Mocesus, standing on level ground, whose wall was so decayed that some part of it had already fallen, and the rest was like to fall. The Emperor Justinian demolished this fort, and built a new and very great wall to the westward of the old fort, on a lofty spot inaccessible to any assailants. Here he built many churches, hospices, public baths, and everything else which belongs to a flourishing city; so that this place came to be regarded as the metropolis, which is the name given by the Romans to the first city of a nation. These were his works in Cappadocia.

V. Along the road leading from the city of Antiochia, now called Theopolis, towards Cilicia, is a suburb named Platanon. Not far from this city was an ancient path, confined in a narrow glen between two mountains, which had been for the greater part washed away by the rains, so as to render it dangerous to travellers proceeding along it. When the Emperor Justinian heard of this, he spent much pains and thought upon it, and at once discovered a remedy for this evil; for at a vast expense he cut down and overcame the difficulties of the mountains in that region for a great distance, so that, beyond everyone's hope and expectation, he made a level and wide carriage-road over what had formerly been precipice, clearly proving that by wise plans and lavish expenditure men can overcome all obstacles. These were his works in that quarter.

There is in Cilicia a city named Mopsuestia,* the work, it is said, of the celebrated ancient prophet (Mopsus). Beside this runs the river Pyramus, which is an ornament to the city, but is only traversed by one bridge. In the course of ages the greater part of this bridge became ruinous, so that it continually threatened to fall, and all who crossed it did so with the fear of death before their eyes. Thus, a work devised by the ancients for men's safety had, through the negligence of those in charge of it, become a source of danger and terror; however, our

---

* Leake's, 'Tour in Asia Minor,' pp. 180, 217. (S.)

Emperor carefully restored all the ruinous parts of the bridge, so as to afford security to those who crossed it, and enabled the city again to take a pride in the river unalloyed with fear.

Beyond this is the city of Adana, round the eastern side of which runs a river named Sarus,* which rises in the mountains of Armenia. The Sarus is a navigable river, and is nowhere fordable on foot. Here in ancient times there had been constructed a large and admirable bridge, in the following manner. In the river were built many piers, formed of large stones of great thickness, extending across the whole width of the river, and rising high above its surface. Above the two central ones rise two lofty arches. These piers, standing in the water, and having to withstand the force of a strong current, had in the course of ages become for the most part ruinous, so that at no distant time it appeared probable that the whole bridge would fall into the river, and every man who crossed it prayed that it might only just hold together until he had done so. However, the Emperor Justinian dug a new channel for the river, into which he diverted its stream for a time, removed the water from the above-mentioned piers, promptly removed the ruinous portions of them, and rebuilt them, after which he turned the river back again into the channel which is called its bed. These were his proceedings here.

The river Cydnus† runs through the midst of the city of Tarsus, and appears to have done no injury to it at any time except once, when it caused great destruction in the following manner: the season was spring-time, and a south wind, which suddenly began to blow with great strength, melted all the snow with which in winter-time the Tarsus Mountains are almost entirely covered. In

* Leake, p. 215. (S.) † Ibid., p. 214.

consequence of this streams of water ran down from every part of those mountains, all the ravines poured down torrents, and numerous springs inundated all the skirts of the Tarsus range. The river Cydnus, swollen high by these waters which were poured into it by its tributaries, and by heavy rains which afterwards fell, overflowed and entirely washed away all the suburbs of Tarsus on the southern side, poured furiously into the city, sweeping away the bridges, which were of slight construction, inundated all the streets and market-places, and even rose as high as the upper stories of the houses. For a night and a day the city remained in this danger and distress, after which the river gradually retired and returned to its usual bed. When the Emperor Justinian heard of this, he devised the following plan. In the first place, he prepared a second channel for the river outside the city, in order that it might there divide its stream, and might only pour half its waters upon the city of Tarsus: next, he built the bridges very much wider, and rendered them too strong to be swept away by the flooded Cydnus. Thus he enabled the inhabitants of the city to dwell in it without alarms or dangers for the future.

VI. These were the works of the Emperor Justinian in Cilicia. At Jerusalem he built a church in honour of the Virgin,* to which no other can be compared. The inhabitants call it the 'new church.' I shall describe what it is like, prefacing my account by the remark that this city stands for the most part upon hilly ground, which hills are not formed of earth, but are rough and precipitous, so as to make the paths up and down them as steep as ladders. All the rest of the buildings in the city stand in one place,

* 'The Virgin of Jerusalem might exult in the temple erected by her imperial votary on a most ungrateful spot, which afforded neither ground nor materials to the architect,' etc., etc.—Gibbon, ch. xl. (S.)

being either built upon the hills, or upon flat and open ground; but this church alone stands in a different position; for the Emperor Justinian ordered it to be built upon the highest of the hills, explaining of what size he wished it to be, both in width and in length. The hill was not of sufficient size to enable the work to be carried out according to the Emperor's orders, but a fourth part

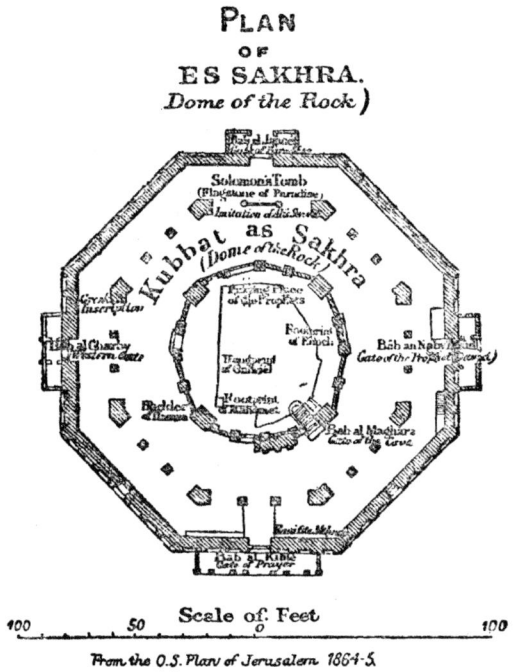

of the church, that towards the south wind and the rising sun, in which the priests perform the sacred mysteries, was left with no ground upon which to rest. Accordingly those in charge of this work devised the following expedient: they laid foundations at the extremity of the flat ground, and constructed a building rising to the same height as the hill. When it reached the summit, they placed vaults upon the walls and joined this building to

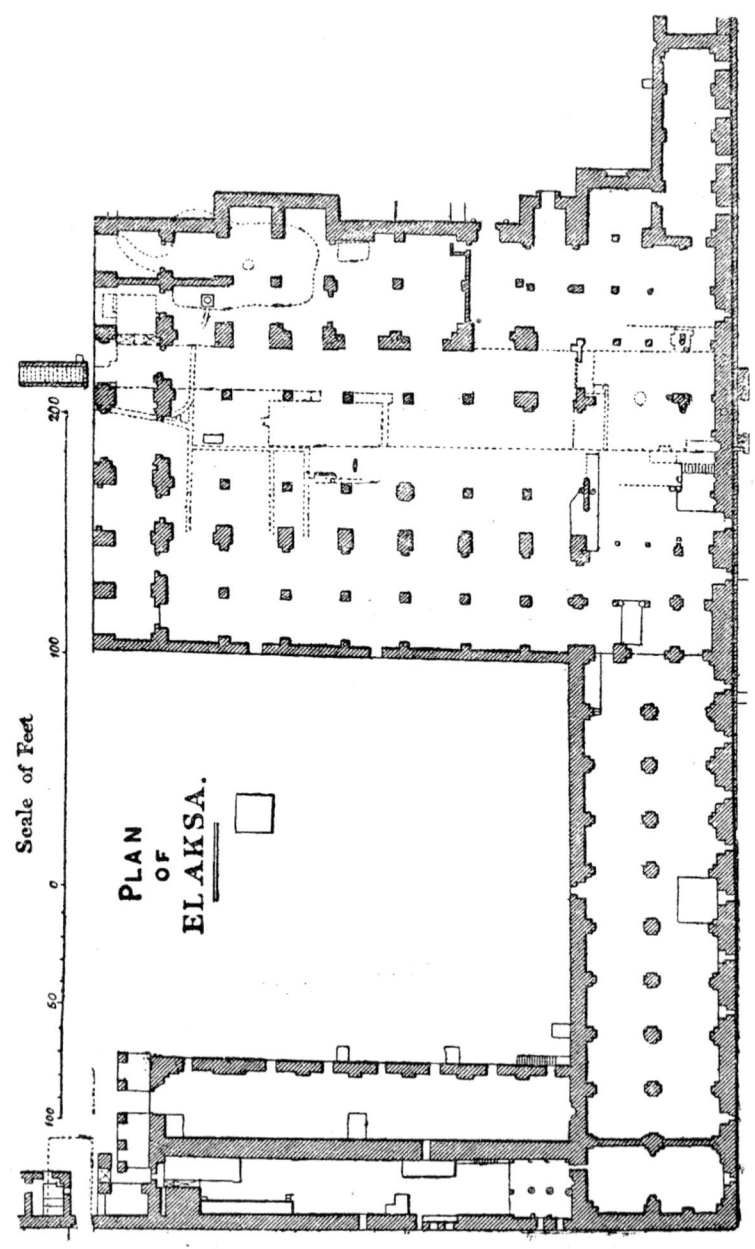

the other foundations of the church; so that this church in one place is built upon a firm rock, and in another place is suspended in the air—for the power of the Emperor has added another portion to the (original) hill. The stones of this substruction are not of the size of those which we are accustomed to see: for the builders of this work, having to contend with the nature of the ground, and being forced to raise a building equal in size to a mountain, scorned the ordinary practices of building, and betook themselves to strange and altogether unknown methods. They cut blocks of stone of enormous size out of the mountains which rise to vast heights in the neighbourhood of the city, cunningly squared them, and brought them thither in the following manner: they built waggons of the same size as these stones, and placed one stone upon each waggon. These waggons were dragged by picked oxen, chosen by the Emperor, forty of them dragging each waggon with its stone. Since it was impossible for the roads leading into the city to take these waggons upon them, they made a passage for them by cutting deeply into the mountains, and thus formed the church of the great length which it was the Emperor's pleasure that it should have. After they had built it of a proportional width they were not able to put a roof upon it. While they were inspecting every grove and place which they heard was planted with tall trees, they discovered a thick wood, producing cedars of enormous height, with which they made the roof of the church, of a height proportional to its length and width. These were the works* which the Emperor Justinian constructed by human power and art, though assisted by his pious confidence, which in its turn reflected honour upon himself, and helped him to carry out his design. This church required to be surrounded on every side with columns, such as in beauty would be

* See Appendix II.

worthy of the main building, and of a size capable of supporting the weight which would be laid upon them. However, the place, from its inland situation at a distance from the sea, and its being entirely surrounded by the precipitous mountains which I have mentioned, rendered it impossible for the builders of the foundation to bring columns thither from elsewhere. While, however, the Emperor was grieving at this difficulty, God pointed out in the nearest mountains a bed of stone of a kind suitable for this purpose, which either had existed there in former times and been concealed, or was then created. Either story is credible to those who regard God as the cause of it: for we, measuring everything by our human strength, think that many things belong to the region of the impossible, while for God nothing whatever is difficult or impossible. The church, then, is supported by a great number of columns brought from this place, of very great size, and of a colour which resembles flame, which stand, some above, some below, and some round the porticos which encircle the entire church, except on the side turned towards the east. Of these columns, the two which stand before the door of the church are of very unusual size, and probably second to no columns in the whole world. Beyond them is another portico, named the Narthex (reed), I suppose because it is narrow; after this is a court of square shape supported by columns of equal size; from this lead interior doors of such grandeur as to show those passing them what a spectacle they are about to meet with. Beyond this is a wonderful porch, and an arch supported on two columns at a great height. Proceeding further, there stand two semicircles, opposite to one another, on each side of the way to the church; while on either side of the other road are two hospices—the work of the Emperor Justinian—one of which is destined for the reception of strangers, while the other is an infirmary for the sick poor. The Emperor Justinian also endowed this Church of the Virgin with large revenues. Such were the works of the Emperor Justinian in Jerusalem.

VII. There is a city in Palestine named Neapolis, which is overhung by a lofty mountain named Gerizim.* This mountain was originally held by the Samaritans, who ascended it at all seasons in order to pray, not that they had ever built a church there, but worshipped and reverenced the summit of the mountain above everything else. Jesus, the Son of God, when in the flesh, went amongst these people, and held a conversation with one of the women of the country. When she inquired of Him about the mountain, He told her that in future times the Samaritans should not worship in this mountain, but that the true worshippers should worship Himself there, alluding to the Christians. In process of time this prophecy came to pass, for it was not possible that the true God should lie. It came to pass in the following manner. In the reign of the Emperor Zeno, the Samaritans sud-

---

* The church is octagonal. On the east side is an apse; on the north the main entrance. On five sides there are small chapels, and on the eighth probably a sixth. There is an inner octagon, which gives the place some resemblance to that of the Dome of the Rock. The only capital uncovered was of a debased Corinthian order. The church is believed to have been built by Justinian *circa* 533.

Plans by Sir C. W. Wilson are given in the *Quarterly Statement* of the Palestine Exploration Fund, 1873, p. 68.

The church is 70·0 inside east and west (inscribed circle of internal octagon). East apse, 15·0 diameter; side chapels, 27·0 long inside, with apses 9·0 diameter.

Said by Procopius to have been erected by the Emperor Zeno, not earlier than 474, to the Blessed Virgin. He says also that Justinian, after 529, built the external wall (9·0 thick) of the court, forming a fortress 180 by 230, with chambers built against the wall inside. One is 11·9 by 14·4 internally (*vide* Plan).—'Palestine Exploration Memoirs,' vol. ii., p. 189, 190. (L.)

denly collected together, and fell upon the Christians in Neapolis, who were keeping the feast called Pentecost in their church, and killed many of them, while they struck

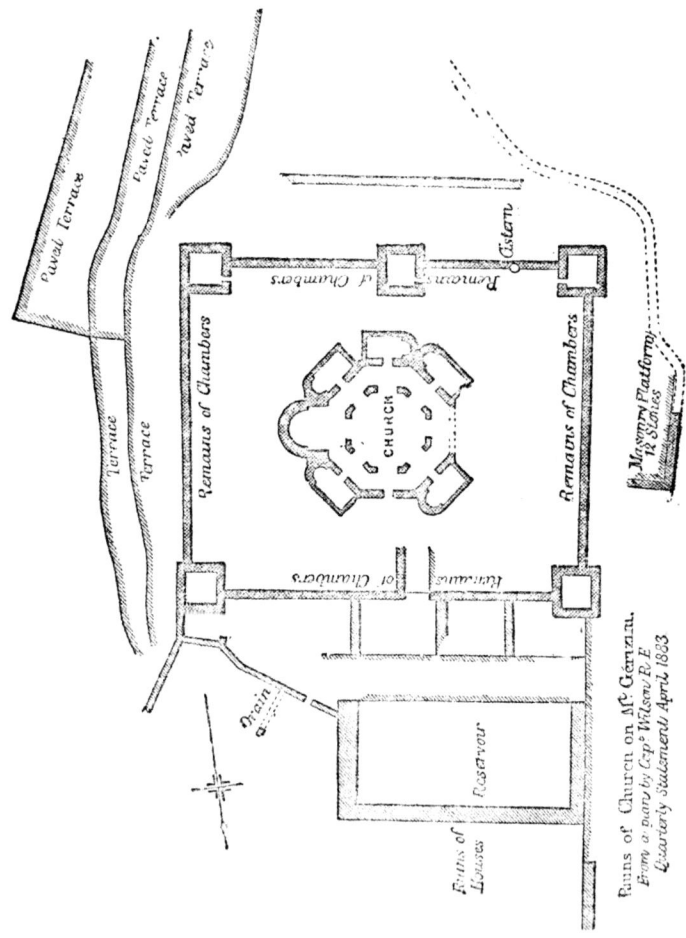

with their swords the Bishop, by name Terebinthius—whom they found standing before the holy table, engaged in celebrating the sacrament—so as, amongst other wounds, to cut off the fingers from his hands, while they insulted the holy mysteries in a manner fit indeed for Samaritans to do, but not fit for us to speak of. This priest shortly afterwards came to Byzantium, into the presence of the then Emperor, to whom he showed what he himself had suffered, described what had taken place, and begged the Emperor to avenge what had been done, reminding him of the prophecy of Christ. The Emperor Zeno, much moved at what had taken place, without delay inflicted a full measure of punishment upon those who had been guilty of this outrage. He drove the Samaritans out of Mount Gerizim, handed it over to the Christians, and built upon the summit a church which he dedicated to the Virgin, which he enclosed with what was indeed called a wall, but which in truth was a dry stone fence. He placed a sufficient number of soldiers as a garrison in the city below, but in the church and its fortification not more than ten. The Samaritans, enraged at these proceedings, were filled with anger, and remained sulky and dissatisfied, though, through fear of the Emperor, they kept silence. In process of time, however, in the reign of Anastasius, the following event took place. Some of the Samaritans, at the instigation of a woman, climbed unexpectedly up the steep face of the mountain, for the road which leads up it from the city was strictly guarded, so that it was impossible for them to ascend by it. Falling suddenly upon the church, they killed the guards who were posted there, and called with a loud voice upon the Samaritans in the city to join them. They, however, fearing the soldiers, were not at all willing to join the conspirators; and not long afterwards the governor of the province (he was named Procopius, of the city of Edessa, an eloquent man) captured those who had been guilty of this outrage, and put them to death. Yet even then the Emperor did not bestow any attention or care upon the fortification; but in our own time the Emperor Justinian, although he has for the most part converted the Samaritans to a better religion, and rendered them Christians, yet, leaving the old wall round the church upon Gerizim in its former condition of loose stones, as I described before, he enclosed it within a second wall, and rendered it altogether impregnable. In this place he also rebuilt five Christian churches which had been burned by the Samaritans. These were his works in this country.

VIII. In the country which was formerly called Arabia, but which now is known as the Third Province of Palestine, a desert tract extends for a great distance, entirely barren of fruits, of water, and of all good things. A precipitous and savagely wild mountain, named Sina, stands close to the Red Sea. It is not necessary at this point in my narrative for me to give a description of these regions, since in my 'History of the Wars' I have given an exact account of the whole of the country near the Red Sea and the so-called Arabian Gulf, and of the tribes of the Auxomite Ethiopians, and the Homerite Saracens. There also I have described how the Emperor Justinian added the palm-grove* to the Roman Empire. I therefore omit to speak of this, that I may not incur the charge of want of taste. In this Mount Sina† dwell monks, whose life is but a careful study of death, and who therefore enjoy without fear the solitude which is dear to them. Since these monks have no desires, but are superior to all human passions, and as they possess nothing and spend no care upon their persons, nor seek for pleasure from anything else whatever, the Emperor Justinian built a

---

* 'The Vale of Palms by the shore of the Red Sea,' Gibbon, ch. xlii.; Stanley, 'Sinai and Palestine,' ed. 12, pp. 20, 85, 519. (S.)

† Full plans, details and descriptions of the fort and church built by Justinian at the foot of J. Mûsa are given in the Ordnance Survey of Sinai. (W.)

church for them, which he dedicated to the Virgin, that they might therein spend their life in continual prayer and service of God. He did not build this church on the summit of the mountain, but a long way below it; for it is not possible for a man to pass the night upon the peak, because at night continuous thunderings and other yet more terrible divine manifestations take place, which overpower men's strength and reason. Here it was that Moses is said to have received the Law from God, and to have brought it away. At the foot of the mountain our Emperor also built a very strong fort, and placed in it a very considerable garrison of soldiers, in order that the barbarian Saracens might not from that point, the country being, as I have said, a desert, secretly invade Palestine. This is what he did here; but what he did in the monasteries, both here and in the remainder of the East, I will now briefly enumerate.

IX. In Jerusalem he restored the following monasteries: that of St. Thalelæus, St. Gregorius, and St. Panteleemon in the desert of Jordan; the hospice at Jericho;* the church of the Virgin at Jericho; the church of the Iberians at Jerusalem; the church of the Lazi in the desert of Jerusalem; the church of St. Mary in the Mount of Olives; the church of the well of St. Elisæus;† the church of

---

* Tell es Sultân and Tellûl Abu el 'Aleik (Roman). Many traces of ruins. The buildings do not appear to have been large or of fine masonry. A pillar-shaft nine inches in diameter, of marble, and fragments of cornices were found; also a capital of the rude Ionic style common in Byzantine buildings, cut in limestone and much weathered.

East and south-east there are extensive ruins on the way to Erîha—mounds, small foundations, and portions of an aqueduct. They do not appear to be of any great antiquity.

Jericho was inhabited in the fourth and fifth centuries, to which date the buildings near the Tell are most probably to be ascribed.— See 'Memoirs, Survey of Western Palestine,' vol. iii., pp. 173, 223. (L.)

† Well of St. Elisæus. May this be Elisha's spring at 'Ain es Sultan? (W.)

Siletheus; the church of the Abbot Romanus. He restored the wall of Bethlehem, and the church of the Abbot Joannes at Bethlehem.

He built cisterns and reservoirs as follows: in the monastery of St. Samuel, a wall and a cistern; in the monastery of the Abbot Zacharia, a cistern; in the monastery of Susanna, a cistern; in the monastery of Aphelius, a cistern; in the

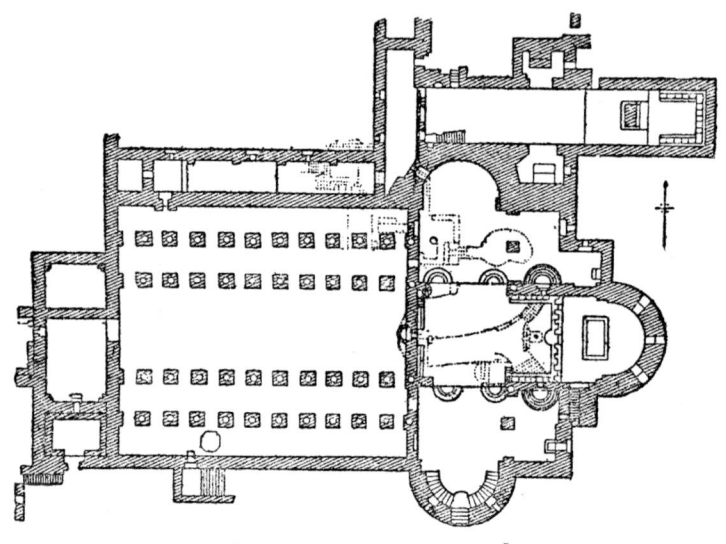

CHURCH AT BETHLEHEM.°

° The church is interesting as being the only basilica of Constantine left standing in Palestine.

The atrium is destroyed, but the basilica, consisting of a nave and four aisles, is almost intact, the original columns and the clerestory walls, with fragments of glass mosaic (of twelfth century), remaining. The basilica measures 87 feet east and west by 75 feet north and south.

At the east end is a transept with north and south apses and an east apse of equal size. The floor of the transept is raised for a width equal to that of the basilica nave (35 feet). The basilica is separated by a wall, erected by the Greeks in 1842, from the transept.—'Palestine Exploration Memoirs,' vol. iii., pp. 83-85.

Notwithstanding the slight notice of this city taken by Procopius, the part taken by Justinian in its adornment is otherwise spoken of in

monastery of St. John beside the Jordan, a cistern;* in the monastery of St. Sergius in the mountain named Cisseron, a cistern; the wall of Tiberias;† the poor-house at Bostra

---

a very striking manner, and its celebrated basilica, usually stated, as above, to have been the work of Constantine, has been assigned in part to Justinian. The eastern part is almost certainly later than Constantine.

'The choir, with its three apses, does not seem to be part of the original arrangement, but to have been added by Justinian when he renovated — Eutychius says rebuilt—the church.'— Fergusson's 'History' (1867), vol. ii., p. 290.

Eutychius' account is thus :

'Jussit etiam Imperator legatum Ecclesiam Bethleemiticam quæ parva fuit diruere, aliamq, amplam, magnam et pulchram fabricare, adeo ut non esset Hierosolymis templum ipsâ pulchrius.

'Perveniens ergo Legatus Hierosolyma, Nosocomium peregrinis condidit, et Ecclesiam Elenæ perfecit, templaque quæ incenderant Samaritani instauravit, nec non Monasteria quam plurima extruxit, dirutâque Ecclesiâ Bethleemiticâ eaudem eo quo jam se habet modo ædificavit.

'Cumque his omnibus absolutis ad Imperatorem reversus esset, ille, describe mihi (inquit) quomodo Ecclesiam Bethleemiticam extruxisti. Quam cum ipsi descripsisset, haud probavit Imperator descriptionem estam nec ullatinus ipsi placuit, quaré valde ipsi iratus. Acceptos (inquit) nummos tibi ipsi congessisti, ædificium autem extruxisti male compactum et Ecclesiam tenebrosam confecisti nullatenus ex mente mea fabricatam, nec consilium meum secutus es. Capiteque ipsumplecti jussit.'

Eutychius adds after Omar's conquest :

'Deinde Bethleem ad eam visendam prefectus cum adesset orationis tempus intra Ecclesiam oravit ad arcum Australem.

'Erat autem arcus totus opere tessellate variegatus. Scripsitque Omar Patriarchæ syngrapham ;—neque mutaretur in eo quiequam.'— Eutychius, ' Pocock's Translation ' (Oxford, 1658), vol. ii., pp. 159, 288.

* The splendid cistern of St. John on Jordan, mentioned by Procopius as the work of Justinian, is still visible in an almost perfect condition. It is 30 feet deep, supported on rows of piers.—' Memoirs,' vol. iii., p. 177.

† Tŭbariya (Tiberias). 'There are the remains of a sea-wall, and of some portions of a city-wall 12·0 thick; many traces of old buildings —at one place foundations which appear to belong to a church.

'Epiphanius, in the fourth century, says that it had long been in-

in Phœnicia; the house of the Virgin at Porphyreon;* the monastery of St. Phoca in the mount; the house of St. Sergius in Ptolemaïs;† the house of St. Leontius at

---

habited, exclusively by Jews. The Sanhedrim came to Tiberias in the middle of the second century. Thence it became the central point of Jewish learning for several centuries. (L.)

'Justinian rebuilt the walls. These were thrown down by an earthquake in 1837.'—'Palestine Exploration Memoirs,' vol. i., p. 419.

'The ruins of the ancient town of Tiberias. A great number of fine granite columns are lying about; also remains of the sea-wall, with towers. Behind the ruins the cliffs rise steeply, with traces of fortifications upon them.'—Palestine Exploration *Quarterly Statement*, 1877, p. 121.

* 'Le Khan dit de Nebi-Younés a été depuis longtemps identifié avec Porphyreon.

'Les dunes paraissent cacher des constructions antiques.

'Quand je passai à Neby-Younés on venait d'ouvrir une de ces dunes, pour en tirer des pierres de construction. On voyait éventrées de jolies chambres, peintes présentant des animaux, des paons affrontés, sous de petits arceaux peints très ornés rappelant la disposition des canons qu'on trouve en tête des beaux évangéliaires Byzantins.

'Il est évident qu'il y eut vers cet endroit une ville assez importante dont la floraison paraît avoir eu lieu surtout à l'époque Chrétienne.'—'Mission de Phénicie dirigée,' par M. Ernest Renan (Paris, Imprimerie Impériale, 1854), p. 510.

Khaifa, a small town at the foot of Mount Carmel. 'Some have held Khaifa to be Sycaminos, and others Porphyreon. There seems to be some grounds for its identity with Sycaminos, but none for its being Porphyreon, nor Gath Hefer (Josh. xix. 13), as Benjamin of Tudela has tried to prove.'—'Journey in Syria and Palestine in 1851-2,' by C. W. M. Van de Velde (8vo., 1854), vol. i., p. 289.

'All that is left of the ancient town of Porphyreon is a single granite column, with a sarcophagus. A Phœnician site has been replaced by a few tamarisks beside a Moslem well.'—Palestine Exploration *Quarterly Statement*, 1874, p. 199.

'The Crusaders called Haifa (at the foot of Carmel) Porphyreon. The real town of this name, which was derived from the purple of the Murex there caught, was eight Roman miles from Sidon towards the north, and just south of the river Tamyras (Nahr Damûr).'—Palestine Exploration *Quarterly Statement*, 1876, p. 188.

† Acre (Ptolemais). 'There are many fragments of Crusading masonry in the town. A small chapel near the sea, of this nature, has

Damascus. In the suburbs of Apamea* he restored the poor-house of St. Romanus; he built the wall of St. Marox; he restored the church of Daphne† in the suburbs of Theopolis; at Laodicea‡ he restored the church of St. John; in Mesopotamia he restored the monastery of St. John, and the monasteries of Thelphrache, Zebinus, Theodotus, Joannes, Sarmathe, Cyrene, Begadacum, and the monastery at Apadnæ, in Isauria.§ He rebuilt the bath and poor-house of the city of Cyricum; the poor-house of St. Conon, and the aqueduct of the same saint in Cyprus; the house of SS. Cosmas and Damianus in Pamphylia;

---

been identified with the Church of St. Andrew. There are also remains of the Hospital of the Knights of St. John and Church of St. John. A plan (given p. 163 of the 'Memoirs') dated 1291 contains notes of many churches and monasteries, but nothing referring to St. Sergius' house.'—' Palestine Exploration Memoirs,' vol. i., pp. 160-167.

* 'A large city of Syria, on the Orontes, called Pella by Seleucus Nicator, who fortified and enlarged it. In the Crusading times it bore the name of Tamieh—now Kŭlat el Medîk. There are large remains of ancient ruins.'—Smith's ' Dictionary of Geography.' (L.)

† This is the celebrated Daphne (now Beit El Ma), near Antioch (Theopolia). (W.)

‡ 'Dr. Robinson identifies the site of Tell Neby Mendeh with the Laodicea of Lebanon (also called Laodicea Cabiosa, Καβιώσα), mentioned by Ptolemy and Polybius—one of six towns founded *circa* 300 B.C. by Seleucus Nicator, in honour of his mother Laodice. It was eighteen M. P. from Emesa (Homs) on the road to Heliopolis (Baalbeck). (W.)

'It is a great mound.

'The principal ruins are on the flat ground east of the mill—the foundations of a building called El Kamû'a, about 50 by 50 feet, with remains of a doorway in the south-east corner. Some broken pillar-shafts lie near, and the walls appear to have been ornamented with pilasters in low relief. The details appear to belong to a late period of classic art.

'These probably are the remains of the Laodicea of later times. This city was the see of a bishop.'—Palestine Exploration *Quarterly Statement*, 1881, pp. 162, 167. (L.)

§ Isauria. A district in Asia Minor to the south of Iconium. (W.)

and the poor-house of St. Michael in the seaport which is called the naval arsenal of the city of Perga, in Pamphylia.

BOOK VI.

I. THE above were the works of Justinian in those regions. What he did at Alexandria was as follows. The river Nile does not flow as far as Alexandria, but, after reaching the city which is named Chæreum,* proceeds to the left, leaving the country about Alexandria. In consequence of this the ancients, in order that the city might not be entirely cut off from the river, dug a deep channel from Chæreum, and succeeded in making a small part of the stream of the river Nile run through it, by which, as by other channels, it discharges its waters into the lake Maria. This channel was nowhere navigable for large ships, but men at Chæreum transfer Egyptian corn from them to boats named *diaremata*, and so bring it to the city, which they can reach by the river which flows through this channel. They store up the corn in the place which the Alexandrians call Phiale. Since it often happened that when the populace rose in revolt, the corn in this place was destroyed, the Emperor Justinian enclosed it with a wall, and prevented any attacks being made upon the corn. These were the works of the Emperor Justinian in this place. However, since the course of our narrative has brought us into Egypt, a country which borders upon Libya, let us describe his works in that country also, since this Emperor found the whole of Libya in the possession of barbarians, and annexed it to the Roman Empire.

* Now probably Karioon, about 15 miles from Alexandria. (L.)

The river Nile, which flows from the Indies into Egypt, divides that land into two portions down to the sea. The land, which is divided by the river, is divided also in name; for the country on the right bank of the river is named Asia, as far as the river Phasis in Colchis, which divides the land of Asia from that of Europe, or indeed to the Cimmerian straits and the river Tanais; for geographers are at issue upon this point, which I have mentioned in the description of the Euxine Sea in my 'History of the Wars.' The country on the left bank of the Nile is called Libya as far as the main ocean, which divides the two continents in the West by interposing an arm between them, which forms our (Mediterranean) Sea. The whole of Libya is divided into various provinces, called, probably, after the name of their inhabitants; but the name of Libya at the present day is applied only to the territory of Pentapolis,* which extends from the frontier at Alexandria as far as the city of Cyrene. In it there is a city, situated at a distance of two days' journey from Alexandria, named Taphosiris,† in which it is said that the Egyptian god Osiris is buried. In this city the Emperor Justinian constructed magistrates' houses, public baths, and other buildings.

II. The greater part of this country of Libya is desert,

---

* 'Discoveries at Cyrene,' by Capt. R. M. Smith, R.E, and Commander E. A. Porcher, R.N. (fol., London, 1864). At page 6 a map of the coast is given, and also a plan, to a small scale, of Ptolemeta, Apollonia, Teuchira and Ben Ghazi (Berenice). The five cities (Pentapolis) of Cyrenaica were Apollonia, Barca, Berenice or Hesperis, Cyrene and Teuchira.

† 'A town in the Libyan Nome, west of the Delta, and about 25 miles from Alexandria. There were probably several places of this name in Egypt, but this appears to have been the most considerable, inasmuch as it was the place where the prefect of Alexandria held the periodical census of the Libyan Nome.'—Smith's 'Dictionary of Geography,' 1857. (L.)

and was almost entirely neglected: yet our Emperor in his watchful care took measures to prevent its incurring any damage from invasion by the neighbouring Moors, for he built two forts and established garrisons in them. One of these forts is named Paratonium, and the other Antipyrgum, which stands near Pentapolis. Pentapolis is distant from Alexandria eight days' journey for a lightly-equipped traveller. In this country of Pentapolis the Emperor Justinian likewise very strongly fortified the city Teuchria,* and rebuilt from its foundations the wall† of Berenice,‡ where he also built a public bath for the use of

---

* 'Tocra, the ancient Teuchria, afterwards called Arsinöe, which, although totally deserted, is still completely enclosed, except on the sea or north side, by walls of uncommon solidity and thickness, strengthened at intervals by quadrangular towers, twenty-six in number, and is entered by two strong-built gateways. . . . The walls were repaired by Justinian, in doing which blocks of stone and marble have been introduced, many bearing Greek inscriptions, which evidently formed part of much older buildings.'—Eng. Cycl., *s.v.* 'Cyrene.' (S.)

A plan of the remains of Taucra or Teuchira is given in Capt. Beechey's 'North Coast of Africa,' p. 388 (4to., 1828). He states, p. 353, that the walls repaired under the Emperor Justinian still remain in a state of perfection which sufficiently proves the solidity of the work. A long account of the city and its walls is given at p. 375, etc. Also in Smith and Porcher's 'Discoveries at Cyrene' (1864), p. 64, where Justinian's walls are particularly mentioned.

† 'Scarcely a vestige of the wall remains.'—Eng. Cycl. *s.v.* 'Bengazi.'

‡ Berenice, about 40 miles to south-west of Barca. Here the ancients placed the gardens of the Hesperides—now Ben Ghazi. (Beechey, p. 314.) Bengazi may be considered as occupying the site of the Berenice of the Ptolemies and of the Hesperis of earlier times; but very few remains now appear above ground to interest the sculptor, the architect or the antiquary.—J. Rennell's 'Herodotus' (4to., London, 1800), p. 154.

Of the ancient city very few remains are now visible. 'At the back of the castle, some foundations may be seen cropping out, but the tomb of a saint prevents any excavations being made.'—Smith and Porcher's 'Discoveries at Cyrene' (1864), p. 13.

'Bengazi, the ancient Berenice, built by Ptolemy Philadelphus.

the citizens; moreover, on the southern frontier of Pentapolis he fortified two monasteries, named Agriolodes and Dinarthion, by which he restrained the barbarians in that quarter from making sudden and unexpected inroads on the Roman territory.

There is in this country a city, named Ptolemaïs,* which in former times was flourishing and populous, but in process of time became almost deserted through want of water; for the greater part of the inhabitants long ago suffered from drought so much that they left it and dispersed in various directions. Now, however, our Emperor has rebuilt the aqueduct which supplied the city with

---

Nothing now remains but its port, which is certainly the best on the coast of Tripoli.' 'On the north there are still to be seen, beyond seamark, the foundations of several large buildings, of stones 8 or 10 feet long and 3 broad, which, by their own weight and being bound by strong cement, have preserved their places.'—Lieut-Col. Playfair, 'Travels in the Footsteps of Bruce' (4to., London, 1877.)

* Ptolemaïs (Ptolemeta), now Dolmeita. V. Beechey, p. 376. He gives, at p. 338, etc., a plan of the city and environs, and also drawings of some of the ruins. The city was something less than a mile in length from north to south, and its breadth from east to west something more than three-quarters. Captain Beechey describes the remains of the walls to the city and harbour, of two theatres, an amphitheatre, and various buildings of more than ordinary consequence. 'Some of the shafts of small columns are spiral and formed of coloured marbles, and may probably be attributed to the time of Justinian, when the city revived under his politic munificence.'

Lieut.-Col. Playfair, 'Footsteps of Bruce' (1877), pp. 288, 289, gives a good account also.

Smith and Porcher, pp. 64, 66, give drawings of ruins. 'At a point nearly opposite the centre of the east wall, the ravine is spanned by the arch of a bridge still standing, which appears to have been built for an aqueduct which we could trace distinctly for some distance from the city. Within the walls the aqueduct led in the direction of enormous reservoirs near the centre of the city.' Messrs. Smith and Porcher describe them as consisting of six chambers, each chamber 100 feet long and 20 broad, arched over. The repairs to the aqueduct and cisterns are ascribed by Procopius to Justinian. (L.)

water, and restored it to its former appearance of prosperity.* The furthest city of Pentapolis upon the western frontier is that of Borium,† where mountains, standing close together, seem to form a barrier which shuts out the enemy from invading the country. The Emperor, finding this city unwalled, enclosed it with a very strong rampart, thus rendering it and the whole of the country round it quite secure for the future.

There are two cities, both of which pass under the same name, being both called Augila.‡ They stand at a distance of about four days' journey from Borium for a lightly equipped traveller, on the southern side of it. They are old cities, and the habits of their citizens are old-fashioned: for all of them, even in my own time, practised the rites of polytheism. Here in ancient times were temples dedicated to Ammon, and to Alexander of Macedon, to whom the inhabitants used to offer sacrifice down to the reign of Justinian, and there was in them a large number of persons called Slaves of the Temple: now, however, our Emperor, who not only provides for the security of the bodies of his subjects, but is also careful to save their souls, took all necessary measures for the benefit of those who dwelt here, making liberal provisions for them in all respects, and above all teaching them the true religion, so that he made them all Christians in a body, and turned them from their pagan ancestral customs. He also built

---

* 'Several of the buildings are partly standing, such as a lofty gateway, an amphitheatre, two theatres, a palace or large building, the inner court of which still retains its tesselated pavement.'—Eng. Cycl. *s.v.* 'Cyrene.' (S.)

† 'The exact position of this S. Borium it is difficult to determine.' —Smith's 'Dictionary of Geography.'

‡ Augila (now Aujilah). 'Its historical importance is considerable, and it is one of those few places whose name has not undergone change since Herodotus wrote.'—Rennell's 'Herodotus,' pp. 568-613 (4to., 1800). (L.)

for them a temple of the Virgin, to serve as a fortress for the safety of the city and of the true religion. These were his works in this quarter.

The city of Borium, lying near the Moorish barbarians, has remained free from imposts down to this time, nor have any gatherers of tribute or taxes visited it since the creation. From ancient times Jews dwelt close to it, and had an ancient temple which they greatly respected and reverenced, as it had, according to tradition, been built by Solomon the King of the Hebrew nation. However, the Emperor Justinian compelled them all to desert their ancestral religion and become Christians, while he turned this temple into a church.

III. Beyond this lie what are called the Great Syrtes. I will explain what their appearance is, and why they have received this name. The shore in this quarter, divided by the inroads of the sea, and washed away by the beating of the waves, seems to retire and to withdraw itself inland, so as to form an immense crescent-shaped gulf. The distance across the mouth of this gulf is forty stadia, while the perimeter of the crescent extends to a distance of six days' journey. The sea forms this gulf by pressing against the mainland; and when a ship is once forced by the wind or the waves within the horns of the crescent, it is thenceforth impossible for it to retrace its course, but it seems dragged along, and always forced further forward. It was, I imagine, from this destruction of ships that the ancients called the place Syrtes. Nor can ships float as far as the shore, for the greater part of the gulf is full of sunken rocks, which make it impossible for ships to float there, so that they are wrecked in the shallows. The crews of these ships can only escape, if they escape at all, in small boats, and reach the land with very great danger. Here is the frontier of the region named Tripolis.

In it dwell Moorish barbarians of Phœnician origin. Here is also a city named Cidama, inhabited by Moors who have long been on terms of friendship with the Romans, and all of whom, by the persuasion of the Emperor Justinian, voluntarily adopted the Christian faith. These Moors are now called Pacati, because they always are at peace with the Romans; for the Romans in the Latin language call peace *pacem*. Tripolis is distant from Pentapolis a journey of twenty days' journey for a lightly equipped traveller.

IV. Beyond this is the city of Leptis Magna,* which in ancient times was great and populous, but since has become almost entirely deserted, having through neglect been mostly buried with sand. Our Emperor rebuilt its walls from the foundation, not, however, enclosing so great an extent as formerly, but much less, in order that the city might not again be exposed to danger, either

---

* Leptis Magna. 'The city appears to have been comprehended within little more than a square half-mile of ground. The actual remains are still sufficient to be somewhat imposing; but they are for the most part so deeply buried under the sand which ten centuries of neglect have allowed to accumulate over them, that plans of them could not be obtained without very extensive excavations. The style of the buildings is universally Roman.' The walls and fortifications, probably restored by Justinian, were finally demolished by the Saracens. From that time the city appears to have been wholly abandoned and its remains employed in the construction of Modern Tripoli. —'North Coast of Africa,' by Beechey (4to., London, 1828), pp. 52, 54.

Lieut.-Col. Playfair, p. 283, describes the remains thus: 'Libidah, the ancient town of Leptis Magna, three days' journey from Tripoli where there are a great extent of ruins, but all in bad taste—chiefly done in the time of Aurelian—indeed very bad. It is said that in the time of Louis XIV. seven monstrous columns of granite or marble were carried from this place into France.' Bruce also states that he saw several statues of good taste which had been deprived of their heads. (L.)

from human enemies or from the sand, by its great size. He left the buried part of the city as it was, covered with heaps of sand, and fortified the rest in the strongest manner. Here he built an admirable church, dedicated to the Virgin, besides four others. In addition to this, he also rebuilt the ruinous palace which formerly existed here, the work of the Emperor Severus the elder, who was born in this place, and left this palace as a memorial of his good fortune.

Having arrived at this part of my narrative, I cannot pass over the great event which took place at Leptis Magna in our time. When Justinian had already come to the throne, and before he had begun the war against the Vandals, the Moorish barbarians called Leucathæ overpowered the Vandals, who were then masters of Libya, and reduced Leptis Magna to an utter desert. Being encamped with their generals upon some hilly ground not far from Leptis Magna, they suddenly beheld a flame of fire in the midst of the city. Supposing that the enemy had entered it, they rushed hurriedly to attack them; but finding no one there, they laid the matter before their prophets, who, interpreting what had taken place, foretold that at no distant time Leptis Magna would be inhabited. Not long afterwards the army of the Emperor arrived, conquered the Vandals and Moors in battle, and gained possession of Tripolis and the rest of Libya. I now return from this digression to my narrative.

In this city the Emperor Justinian built public baths, rebuilt the walls from their foundations, and gave both the baths and all other public buildings an appearance worthy of a city. Moreover, he induced the neighbouring barbarians, named Gadabitani, who up to this time were entirely given up to the Greek form of paganism, to become zealous Christians, as they are at this day. He also fortified the city of Sabaratha, in which he built a most notable church.

In the further part of this country there are two cities, named Tacapa* and Girgis, between which lies the lesser Syrtis. Here every day a wonderful phenomenon takes place. The sea, pent up in a narrow place, forms there a crescent-shaped gulf, such as I described in the other Syrtis. Here the sea flows into the mainland for a distance of more than eight days' journey for a lightly equipped traveller, and towards evening retires again, leaving the shore there dry, like any other sea-beach. Sailors bound for this land, which at times becomes sea, sail in the ordinary manner as far as they are able in the day-time, but towards nightfall prepare to pass the night on dry land. They carry long poles on purpose, and as soon as they suspect that the waters are about to ebb, they take these poles in their hands, and without any hesitation leap out of the ship. At first they swim, but afterwards, when the water does not reach above their faces, they stand on their feet, and sticking the points of their poles into the ground, which by this time is, or shortly will be, dry, they fix them upright underneath their ship, supporting it on either side, that it may not be damaged by falling to one side or the other. Early on the following morning the land is again covered by the waves of the sea, which raises the ships and causes them to float; then the sailors take up their poles and sail on again. This proceeding never varies, but this interchange of the elements takes place every day.

---

* Tacape. 'Gabes: this was the Epichus of Sylax and the Tacape of other ancient geographers; where we have a heap of ruins with some beautiful granite pillars still standing. These are all square and about 12 feet long, and such as I have not met with in any other part of Africa.—Shaw's 'Travels in Barbary,' p. 113. (L.)

V. After Tripolis and the Syrtis, let us proceed to the rest of Libya. We must begin with Carthage, which is the largest and most important of the cities in this country, prefacing our description by observing that when Genseric and the Vandals possessed Africa, there occurred to them a destructive idea worthy of barbarians; for they imagined that they would be better off if all the towns in this country had no walls, so that the Romans might not occupy any of them to their disadvantage. They accordingly at once pulled down all the walls to their very foundation; for all barbarians, as a rule, most quickly devise and most promptly execute any plans which they form for the injury of the Romans. The walls of Carthage and some few other places alone were left, which they did not care to keep in repair, but allowed to be ruined by age. However, the Emperor Justinian, against the advice of all men, who shrank in terror from the enterprise, and only led on and assisted by God, sent Belisarius with an army to Libya, took Gelimer, and destroyed the power of the Vandals, killing many of them and making the rest prisoners of war, as I have recounted in my 'History of the Wars.' He rebuilt all the ruined fortifications in Libya, and himself built many new ones.

First of all, he gave his attention to Carthage,* which

* Carthage. Shaw, p. 81, etc., of his 'Travels in Barbary,' describes the remains of Carthage existing in his time (*circa* 1750), in particular the great cistern (of which he gives a plan at p. 75), 'which had very little suffered,' and 'the famous aqueduct, a great part whereof is still standing:'—'We see—a long range of its arches, all of them intact, 70 feet high, supported by columns 16 feet square. . . . the channel being high and broad enough for an ordinary person to walk in.'

Bruce says, 'We passed ancient Carthage, of which little remains but the cisterns, the aqueduct, and a magnificent flight of steps leading up to the Temple of Esculapius.' He gives (p. 130) a drawing of the aqueduct, which Col. Playfair describes 'as one of the greatest works

now, as is right, is named Justiniana. He rebuilt the whole of its ruined walls, and dug a trench encircling it, which did not previously exist; he also built churches, one dedicated to the Virgin, which is in the palace, and one outside the palace dedicated to St. Prima, one of the local saints. He built porticos on both sides of what is called the Maritime market-place, and a noble public bath, which he named the Baths of Theodora, after the name of the Empress. He also built a monastery on the sea-shore within the walls, close to the harbour, named Mandracium, which he enclosed with a strong wall and formed into an impregnable fort.

These were the works of Justinian at New Carthage, In the country near it, which is called the Proconsulate. there was an unwalled city named Baga,* which was liable to be taken by barbarians, not only if they marched

---

the Romans ever executed in North Africa.' 'It was destroyed by the Vandals, restored by Belisarius, the general of Justinian. On the expulsion of the Byzantines it was once more cut off, restored by the Arabs, again destroyed by the Spaniards, and finally restored by the present Bey, Sidi Saduk, at a cost of 13,000,000 francs.'—Lieut.-Col. Playfair in 'Footsteps of Bruce,' p. 128.

* Baga. 'The city of Beja or Bay-jah, which by the name and situation should be the Vacca of Sallust, the Oppidum Vagense of Pliny, the ΒΑΓΑ of Plutarch, and the Vaccensium ordo Splendissimus, as the title runs in an imperfect inscription.' 'Bay-jah keeps up the character that Sallust gives his Vacca of being a town of great trade.' 'The walls are raised out of the ancient materials.'—Shaw's 'Travels in Barbary,' p. 92.

'The ancient city was surrounded by a wall, flanked by square towers—no doubt this was originally constructed by the Byzantines—but were allowed by the Arabs to fall into decay. The only part in a relative state of preservation is the Kasba, a great part of which seems to me the original construction of Belisarius or Solomon.' It contains 'a large and lofty hall, about 15 paces long and 10 wide, with a vaulted roof supported on two square pillars.'—Lieut.-Col. Playfair, p. 234. (L.)

especially to attack it, but even if they passed near it. This place the Emperor Justinian enclosed with a strong wall, thus raising it to the rank of a city, and one, too, which was capable of affording security to its citizens, who, having met with such favour, named the city Theodorias, in honour of the Empress. He also built a fort in this country, named Tucca.

VI. In Byzacium is a city by the sea-side, named Adrumetus,* which in ancient times was great and populous, so that it had the name and repute of being the chief city in this country, because it was the first in size and in prosperity. The Vandals demolished the walls of this city, that the Romans might not be able to hold it against them, so that it was exposed to the attacks of the Moors, who ravage that country; however, the Libyan inhabitants provided for their own safety as far as they were able, by piling up the ruins of their walls and joining their houses to one another, by which means they were able to offer a precarious resistance to their assailants. Their safety, however, hung by a thread, and was very uncertain, as they were at war with the Moors and neglected by the Vandals. When, however, the Emperor Justinian, in the course of the war, became master of Libya, he built a wall of considerable size round this city, established in it a sufficient garrison of soldiers, and enabled the inhabitants to be confident of safety and to disregard all their foes. For this reason they call it Justiniana to the present day, thus repaying their debt of gratitude to the Emperor,

---

* Adrumetus. 'Herkla—the Heraclea of the lower empire, the Justiniana of the middle, and the Adrumetum of the earlier ages.' 'It appears to have been little more than a mile in circuit.' 'That part of the promontory which formed the port seems to have been walled in quite down to the seashore; but the rest of it, to a distance of a furlong from thence, does not discover the least traces of ruins.'— Shaw's 'Travels in Barbary,' pp. 105, 106. (L.)

and showing their loyalty towards him by the adoption of his name, for they had no other means of repaying the kindness of the Emperor, as he wished for no other return than this. On the shore of Byzacium there is another place named Caputvada* by its inhabitants. It was at this place that the Emperor's army first landed when it proceeded against Gelimer and the Vandals. Here, also, that marvellous and ineffable gift was bestowed by God upon the Emperor, which I have described in my 'History of the Wars.' The country being altogether waterless, the Roman army suffered greatly from thirst, whereupon the earth, which formerly had always been dry, sent forth a fountain at the place where the soldiers had formed their camp. For when they dug, the water burst forth, and the land, divesting itself of its natural barrenness, changed its nature and became moist with sweet water. Here, therefore, they encamped and passed the night, and marching forth in battle array the next day, to cut the matter short, gained possession of Libya. The Emperor Justinian therefore, in order to erect a perpetual memorial of this gift of God, who when He pleases can make the most difficult things easy, at once determined to form this place into a city, with a strong wall, and adorned with everything else worthy of a city. The Emperor's wish was fulfilled. The wall and city were built, and the fortunes of this open field were suddenly altered. The rustics, throwing away the plough, dwell as citizens, and no longer live a country, but a town life; for they meet together

* Ca-poudia, the Caput Veda of Procopius, the Ammonis Promontorium of Strabo, and the Promontorium Brachodes of Ptolemy—a low narrow strip of land which stretches itself a great way into the sea. Upon the very point of it we have the ruins of the city that was built there by Justinian, where there is likewise a high round watch-tower.' —Shaw's 'Travels in Barbary,' p. 111. (L.)

there daily, deliberate upon their own affairs, buy and sell in the market with one another, and perform all the other functions which distinguish the inhabitants of a city.

These were his works on the seashore of Byzacium. In the interior, on the frontier which borders on the barbarian Moors, very strong fortresses are built to hold them in check, in consequence of which they are no longer able to overrun the empire, for he enclosed each of the cities upon that frontier, which are named Mamma, Telepta, and Cululius, with very strong walls, built a fort which the inhabitants name Aumetera, and established in them trustworthy garrisons of soldiers.

VII. In the same manner he ensured the safety of the country of Numidia by fortifications and garrisons of soldiers. I shall now enumerate each of these in detail. There is a mountain in Numidia called Aurasius,* the like of which does not exist anywhere else in the world. In the first place, it is lofty and precipitous, and extends for a distance of about three days' journey; it is also inaccessible, all the ascents to it being barred by precipices. When, however, one has reached the top, the ground is a rich soil, smooth, and with easy roads, fair pastures, parks planted with trees and all kinds of herbs. Fountains spring out from the crags; there are quiet pools, rushing rivers with

---

* 'Of the Vandals chosen by Belisarius, the far greater part, in the honours of the Eastern service, forgot their country and religion. But a generous band of four hundred obliged the mariners, when they were within sight of the Isle of Lesbos, to alter their course: they touched at Peloponnesus, ran ashore on a desert coast of Africa, and boldly erected on mount Aurasius the standard of independence and revolt.' —Gibbon, ch. xliii. (S.)

Aurasius. The Auris Mountains. The inhabitants still retain some marked peculiarities which distinguish them from the surrounding people. (W.)

masses of broken water, and, what is strangest of all, the crops and fruit-trees on this mountain produce twice as much as any other part of Libya. Such is the mountain of Aurasium, which was originally held by the Vandals, whom the Moors dispossessed, and dwelt there until the Emperor Justinian drove them out and annexed it to the Roman Empire. To prevent the barbarians returning thither and doing mischief, he fortified the cities in the neighbourhood of this mountain, which he found deserted and without walls; and having, besides them, built two forts, and established there a sufficient garrison of soldiers, he left the barbarians of that country no hope of making a successful attack upon Aurasius. He also built impregnable fortifications in the remainder of Numidia. These were his works in this country.

There is a city in the island of Sardo, which is now called Sardinia, which the Romans call the Fort of Trajan; this Justinian enclosed with a wall, which it did not formerly possess.

Near Gades, by one of the pillars of Hercules, on the right hand, on the shore of Libya, was once a fort named Septon,* which had been built by the Romans in ancient times, but had been neglected by the Vandals and had perished through age. This place our Emperor Justinian made strong by a wall and a garrison. In it also he built a noble church dedicated to the Virgin, thus dedicating to her the beginning of the empire, and rendering this fort impregnable to all mankind in that quarter.

So much for this. No one can any longer doubt, but it is now clear to all mankind that the Emperor Justinian strengthened the empire, not only with fortifications, but also with garrisons, from the eastern frontier to the setting

---

* Septem or Ceuta.

sun, which are the limits of the Roman dominion. Such of the buildings of Justinian as I have been able to discover, either by having seen them myself, or by hearing them described by those who have seen them, I have as far as I am able described in this work; but I am well aware that I have omitted to speak of many others, which have either escaped my notice by their great number or remain altogether unknown to me; so that anyone who turns his attention to searching them all out and describing them in a book will have the advantage of having performed a useful work, and will gain for himself the reputation of a man of taste.

APPENDIX I.

PROCOPIUS'S description of Justinian's work at Constantinople is so full and detailed that it would appear to be complete. But it omits one church built by the Emperor, viz., that of the Saviour, to which was attached the Monastery of the Chora, now known as the Mosque Kahireh, or Kahriyeh.

The history of this church is thus given in Ducange:

'Chora seu Χώρα monasterium ita appellatum, condiderat Justinianus et cum præ vetustate concidisset aliud a fundamentis extruxit Alexii Imperatoris socrus Andronici Ducæ conjux.

'Denique cum ruinam rursum minaretur, illud reædificavit Theodorus Metochita Magnus Logotheta, imperante Andronico Palæologo Seniore.

'Hæc omnia sic narrat Nicephorus Gregoras, lib. ix.: "Divertit e regione et in vicinia (domus suæ) in sacro scilicet Choræ Monasterio, quod ipse magnis ante sumptibus vetustate ruinosum instauravat. Exstructum enim olim fuerat a Justiniano Imperatore forma oblonga: deinde cum vetustate usque ad ima concidisset, aliud a fundamentis templum, ea qua nunc forma cernitur, Alexii Comneni Imperatoris socrus condidit sed cum rursus ruinam minitaretur, hic medio templo excepto, omnia liberali manu pene instauravit. Metochitam hujus monasterii instauratorem rursus prædicat, lib. viii." '—Ducange, iv., p. 126.

An inscription over the south door of the church states

that the monastery was outside the walls of Constantine; that the church was rebuilt by Justinian; again, from its foundations, in the time of Alexis Komnenos; and again rebuilt by Theodore the Metochite.

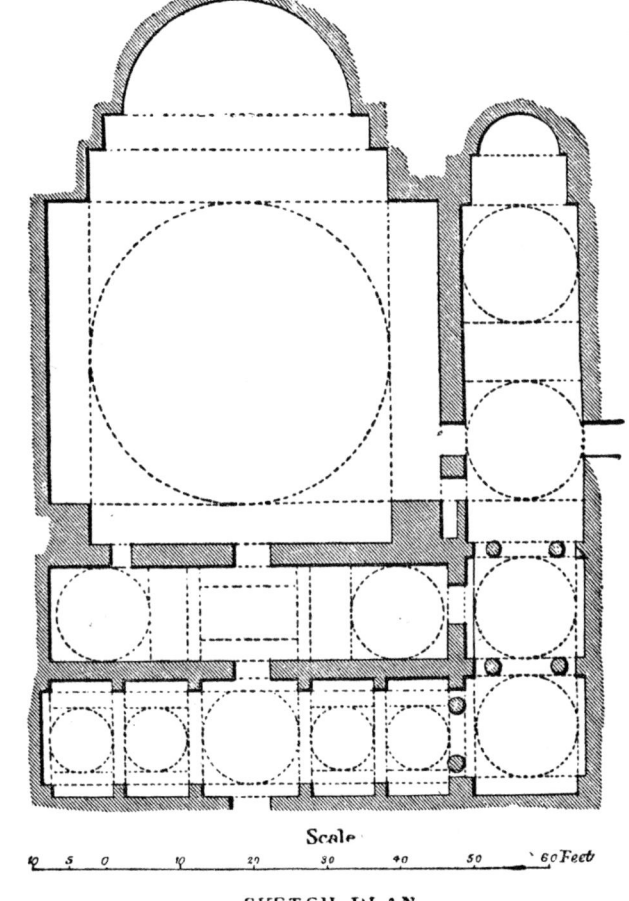

SKETCH PLAN

The well-known antiquary, Mons. Texier, describes it thus in a detailed MS. account of 'Constantinople,' fol. *n. d.*, in the library of the R. Institute of Architects:

'Kahrije, corruption du Grec της χωρας.

'Le premier fondateur de cette église fut Justinian; et Theodore Metochite, grand chancelier des Autels d'Andronice Paléologue n'en fut que le rénovateur. Le cloître est souvent cité dans les auteurs Byzantines comme lieu d'exil pour les religieux, et au dernier temps de l'empire on conserva dans l'église le portrait célèbre de la Madone qui avait été peint par St. Luke.' A description of it is also given in Salzenberg's 'Alt-Christliche Baudenkmale von Constantinopel' (Berlin, 1854), p. 36.

The latest account is given by the Rev. Charles G. Curtis, in the 'Encyclopædia Britannica,' 9th edition, s.v. 'Constantinople:'

'The monastery to which this church of the Saviour belonged was Μονὴ τῆς χώρας, or, as we say, "in the fields." This was an ancient establishment, and its church, the oldest church in the city, dates from the third century.

'A gem of beauty still, even in its decay, rich with mosaic of the fourteenth century, of a style purer and more refined than that which is more often seen and admired at Ravenna and Palermo. In this church alternately with the Hodegetria was kept the Holy Robe of the Virgin, which was wont to be carried in procession when the walls were threatened.' The sketch-plan engraved was made by T. H. L. in 1884. An elevation of the exterior is given in C. Daly's 'Revue' (1840), p. 13. (L.)

APPENDIX II.

CHURCH of the Virgin, Jerusalem:

The description by Procopius of this church is very detailed; but the great alterations and destruction of buildings throughout the Harem area since his time make it extremely difficult to arrive at a correct understanding of his account, or to identify any portion of the church with existing buildings. It is usually supposed to have occupied the site of the present Mosque El Aksa, the entrances to which the Duc de Vogüé believes to be remains of Justinian's church.

The questions as to the church are involved, to a considerable extent, with those relating to the date and authorship of the Dome of the Rock, which has usually been assigned to the Caleph Abd-el-Melek; but the late Mr. Fergusson, whose great architectural knowledge is undisputed, maintained that it was no other than Constantine's Church of the Holy Sepulchre, and that the church described by Procopius was not on the site of El Aksa, but at the eastern angle of the temple area, and now utterly destroyed.

The subject, already sufficiently complicated, has been rendered still more so by a theory brought forward in 1882, by the well-known Professor Sepp, to the effect that the Dome of the Rock was not constructed by Constantine nor by Abd-el-Melek, but by Justinian.

The question is much more difficult to decide than may at first sight appear; and I confess that after having, for some years past, carefully collected the various documents on the subject, including the valuable translations published by my friend the late Professor Palmer, of Arabic historians, and having subsequently visited Jerusalem and studied the subject on the spot, with the kind assistance of Dr. Chaplin and others, I find that there are so many points to be cleared up, that I should not like to offer a definite opinion on the several disputed points until after another visit, which I hope to make shortly, to Jerusalem. My present views, so far as I may venture to put them forward, are in accordance with those of De Vogüé, Sir C. Warren and Captain Conder, viz., that the Dome of the Rock was built by Abd-el-Melek. (L.)

INDEX.

A.

Abbot Romanus, Church of the, 147
Abbot Joannes, Church of the, 148
Abbot Zacharia, Monastery of, 148
Aborrhas, River, 54, 55, 57
Abydos, 121, 128
Acacius, Church of, 22
Acarnania, 93
Ad Aquas, 111
Adana, 137
Adina, 113
Adriatic Sea, 90
Adrianopolis, 93
Adrumetus, 163
Aëdabe, 112
Ægean Sea, 24
Ægistum, 114
Ænus, 121, 122
Ætolia, 93
Agriolodes, Monastery of, 155
El Aksa, 140
Alexandria, 128, 152, 153
Almus, 111
Almyris, 114
Albinum, 113
Alustus, 88
Amasea, 86
Amida, 40, 51, 53, 73, 75, 77, 78, 79, 82
Ammodius, 45
Anaplus, 24, 29, 30, 31
Anastasiopolis, 122
Anchialus, 89
Annucas, 57
Antiphorus, 59
Antipyrgum, 154
Antiochia, 68, 69, 70, 71, 136
Ant, the, 116
Antoninus, Baths of, 131, 132
Apadnæ, Monastery of, 151
Apadnæ, 53
Apamea, 151
Aphelius, Monastery of, 148
Apostles, Church of, 20
Artaleson, 80
Archangel, Temple of the, 33
Arcadius, 15
Arcadius, Baths of, 36
Arcon, 81
Argyronium, 33

Armenia, Lesser, 81
Armenia, 28, 73, 75, 77, 79, 80, 81, 82, 83, 84, 89
Armenia, Greater, 74, 75, 79, 82
Armata, 111
Arxanes, 77
Asia, 25
Asthianene, 79
Atachæ, 53
Athyra, 116
Athens, 96, 98
Augusta, 112
Augila, 156
Augustæum, 13, 34
Aumetera, 165
Aurasius, Mount, 165

B.

Baga, 162
Baiberdon, 81
Baleæ, 96
Banasymeon, 53
Bara, 53
Barchon, 86
Barbalissus, 65
Batnæ, 61
Bederiana, 91, 92
Begadacum, Monastery of, 151
Belabitis, 76
Bellurus, 122
Bergonovore, 111
Bergus Altus, 111
Berenice, 154
Bethlehem, 148
Bidamas, 57
Bigrane, 111
Bismideon, 57
Bithynia, 129, 133, 134
Bizana, 81, 83, 84
Blachernæ, 16, 26
Black Gulf, 119
Bœotia, 96
Bononia, 111
Borium, 156, 157
Bosporus, 88
Bostra, in Phœnicia, 150
Brochi, 29
Byrthum, 53
Byzantium, 15, 16, 18, 20, 24, 26, 29, 31, 33, 38, 114, 117, 123, 129, 134, 145
Byzacium, 163, 164

C.

Cæsarea, 98, 135
Callipolis, 121
Callinicum, 57, 61, 64
Campses, 109
Candidiana, 113
Cantabazates, 109
Cappadocia, 135, 136
Caputvada, 164
Caput-bovis, 109
Carrhæ, 57, 61
Carthage, 161
Cassandria, 99
Castoria, Lake, 97
Castramartis, 112
Cebres, 111
Centauropolis, 98
Cena, 86
Ceras, Gulf of, 24
Chæreum, 152
Chalcis, 71, 72, 98
Chalce, The Palace of, 34, 35
Cherson, 88
Chora, Church of, 40
Chersonesus, 119, 120, 121
Ciberis, 121
Cidama, 158
Cilicia, 136, 138
Cimmerian Straits, 153
Ciphæ, Fort, 53
Circesium, 55, 57
Citharizon, 77, 79
Clisuræ, 79, 87, 96
Colonia, 81
Commagene, 61
Constantinople, 13, 34, 37, 40, 115, 118, 128
Constantina, 54
Corinth, 96
Coracii, 96
Corzane, 79
Corde, 45
Couriers' Lodgings, 131
Cratiscara, 92
Crissæan Gulf, 93
Crispas, 111
Cucarizon, 81
Cululius, 165
Cupus, 109
Cydnus, River, 137, 138
Cyntodemus, 113
Cynton, 113
Cyprus, 151
Cyricum, 151
Cyrene, Monastery of 151
Cyrus, 71, 72
Cyrene, City of, 153

D.

Dabanæ, 53
Dacia, 108, 109
Damascus, 110
Danube, River, 89, 91, 92, 108, 109, 110, 112, 113, 114
Daphne, 113, 151
Dardani, 92
Daras, a village, 40, 41, 42, 43, 47, 48, 49, 51, 52, 53, 83
Dausaron, 57
Demetrias, 97
Deuteron, 17
Dimarthion, Monastery of, 155
Diocletianopolis, 97
Ditch of Germanus, 81
Ditch of Longinus, 86
Dorostolus, 113
Doru, 88
Dorticum, 111
Draco, River, 130
Ducepratum, 109

E.

Echinæum, 97
Edessa, 57, 58, 59, 60, 145
Elæus, 119, 121
Ephesus, 127, 128
Epirus, 93
Epidamnus, 91
Episcopia, 116
Eryma, 112
Eubœa, Island, 98
Euphratesia, 65, 67
Euphrates, River, 53, 56, 61, 63, 64, 65, 75, 81, 82
Euripus, Strait of, 99
Europus, 65
Eurœa, 93
Eutropius, 39
Euxine Sea, 24, 29, 32, 86, 89, 153

F.

Forum of Constantine, 34, 35
Forty Martyrs, 81
Fort of the Emperors, 53
Fountain, The, 16
Forts, Lists of, 100-107, 123-126

G.

Gabula, 65
Gades, 166
Galatia, 134
Gerizim, 143, 144, 145, 146
Germana, 92
Girgis, 160
Golden Gate, 17, 33
Gomphi, 97

INDEX. 175

Gombes, 111
Greece, 93, 96, 98
Great Syrtes, 157

H.

Halicaniburgus, 111
Hebdomon, 23, 31
Hellespont, 119, 128, 133
Helena, 129
Hemerius, 65
Hera, Temple of, 17
Heraclea, 96, 118, 119
Hieriphthon, Fort, 53
Hieron, 33
Hiereum, } 17
  or
Heræum, } 38, 39
Hierapolis, 66
Horn, The, 29
Hormisdas, 18, 34
House of Ares, 35
Huns, Fort of the, 112
Hypata, 96

I.

Iatron, 113
Iberians, Church of, 147
Ibida, 114
Illyrisis, 79
Illyria, 96, 110, 112, 113
Ionian Gulf, 90
Irene, Church of, 14, 27
Isauria, 151
Iscum, 112
Isidorus, 15
Isthmus of Corinth, 93
Ister, River, 108, 114
Italy, 36, 67, 88

J.

Jecundiana, 38
Jerusalem, 147
Jericho, Hospice at 147
Joannes, Monastery of, 151
Jordan, Desert of, 147
Judæus, 111
Julian, Port, 23
Juliopolis, 134
Justinopolis, 92, 93
Justiniana Secunda, 92
Justiniana Prima, 91
Justiniana (Carthage), 162, 163

K.

King's Palace, 18

L.

Laccobergus, 111

Laodicea, 151
Lapidaria, 112
Larissa, 98
Lazi, Church of the, 147
Lazica, 87
Lebanon, 73
Lederata, 109
Leontarium, 96
Leptis Magna, 158, 159
Libya, 36, 67, 127, 152, 153, 159, 161, 166
Litorata, 109
Longiniana, 111
Losorium, 87
Lucernariaburgum, 112
Lutararizon, 81
Lurnes, 53
Lysiormum, 81

M.

Macedon, 74, 99, 102
Mæotic Lake, 87, 88
Magne Kahireh, Church of, 168, 169
Magdalathum, Fort, 57
Mamma, 165
Mandracium (Harbour), 162
Marathon, 98
Mareburgus, 111
Maria, Lake, 152
Martyr Anthimus, Church of, 27
Martyr Eugenius (Aqueduct), 86
Martyr Menas, Church of, 33
Martyr Menæus, Church of, 33
Martyr Mocius, Church of, 23
Martyropolis, 51, 77, 78, 79
Martyr St. Panteleëmon, Church 32
Martyr Thecla, Church of, 23
Martyr Thyssus, Church of, 23
Maxentius, 113
Maximianopolis, 122
Melitene, 28, 82
Mesopotamia, 53, 57, 61, 76
Metropolis, 97
Mocesus, 135
Mochadius, 33
Mocatiana, 111
Mopsuestia, 136
Mount Hæmus, 123
Mount Pelion, 98
Myropole, 96
Mysia, 114

N.

Naïsopolis, 92
Neapolis, 143, 144
Neocæsarea, 65, 67
New Epirus, 93, 100

Nicæa in Bithynia, 130
Nicomedia, 131
Nicopolis, 81, 93
Nile, River, 152, 153
Novæ, 109
Novum, 111
Numidia, 165
Nymphius, River, 77

O.

Octavum, 108
Old Epirus, 23
Onopnictes, 70
Onos, 111
Orocassias, 69, 70
Oronon, 85
Orontes, River, 68, 69
Osrhoëne, 61, 80

P.

Palmyra, 127
Pallene, Peninsula of, 99
Palestine, 72, 143, 147
Palmatis, 113
Palatiolum, 112
Pamphylia, 152
Pantalia, 92
Paratonium, 154
Peloponnesus, 97
Pentacomia, 65
Pentapolis, 153, 154, 155, 156
Peneus, River, 98
Persian Armenia, 85
Perga, 152
Persia, 51, 52
Perinthus, 118
Petra, 87
Petrius, 81
Pharsalus, 97
Phœnice, 93
Phœnicia, 73
Phasis in Colchis, River, 153
Phison, 79
Phiale, 152
Philippopolis, 123
Philæ, 57
Photica, 93
Phrygia, 133
Phthia, 98
Picnus, 109
Pityous, 87
Platanon, 136
Platæa, 96
Plotinopolis, 123
Pontem, 110
Pontes, 109, 110
Ponteserium, 111
Potidæa, 99
Ptolemais, 155

Proochthus, 29
Propontis, 36
Putedin, 111
Pyramus, River, 136
Pyramids, the, 40
Pythia, 134

Q.

Quesoris, 113
Quimedaba, 92

R.

Ratiaria, 111
Rhabdium, 51, 52
Rhœdestus, 119
Rhasis, 53
Rhegium, 115
Rhesias, 23
Rhecius, River, 99, 100
Rhipalthæ, 53
Rhizeum, 87
Rhodope Mountains, 122, 123
Ripensis, 109
Roman Empire, 29, 43, 54, 56, 85
   88, 94, 117, 146, 152
Rumisiana, 92

S.

Sabaratha, 160
Saccus, 96
Sakhra, es (Dome of the Rock), 139
Saltopyrgus, Fort, 11
Sangaris, River, 133
Saphchæ, 79
Sarmathe, Monastery of, 151
Sardica, 92
Sardo, Island (Sardinia), 166
Sarus, River, 137
Satala, 80
Sauræ, 53
Schamalinichon, 85, 86
Scirtus, River, 58
Scythia, 114
Sebastia, 81
Sebastopolis, 87, 88
Securisca, 113
Selybria, 118
Semiramis at Babylon, 10
Sergius and Bacchus, SS., 14, 18, 19,
Sergiopolis, 65
Sergius, 65
Sestos, 121, 128
Siberis, River, 134
Sicibida, 112
Siletheus, Church of, 147
Sinæ, 53
Singedon, 109
Sinai, Mount (close to Red Sea), 146
Siphris, 53

INDEX.

Sisilisson, 86
Sisauranum, Fort, 52
Smargdis, 53
Smornes, 109
Sophanene, 77, 78, 79
St. Agathonicus, Church of, 23
Stauris, 70
St. Anne, Church of, 17
Stadium, 40
St. Bartholomew, Church of, 45, 51
SS. Cosmas and Damianus in Pamphylia, House of, 151
SS. Cosmas and Damianus, Church of, 26
St. Conon, Poor-house of, 151
St. Cyrillus, 114
St. Elisæus, Church of the Well of, 147
St. George the Martyr, Church of, 81
St. Gregorius, 147
Stiliburgus, 111
St. John, Church of, 151
St. John, Monastery of, 149, 151
St. John the Baptist, Church of, 30
St. James, Church of, 33
St. John the Apostle, Church of, 127
St. Laurentius the Martyr, Church of, 26
St. Leontius, House of, 150
St. Marox, 151
St. Michael the Archangel, Church to (Antioch), 71
St. Michael, Poor-house of, 152
St. Michael the Archangel, at Byzantium, Church of, 17, 29, 31, 134
St. Mary, Church of, 147
Stork, the, 33
St. Phoca, Monastery of, 150
St. Plato the Martyr, Church of, 23
SS. Priscus and Nicolaus, Church of, 26
SS. Peter and Paul, 18
St. Panteleëmon, 147
St. Romanus, Poor-house of, 151
St. Sergius, Monastery of, 149
St. Samuel, Monastery of, 148
St. Sophia, Church of, 4, 11, 14, 15, 21, 34, 51
St. Theodorus, Church of, 23
St. Theodota, 23
St. Tryphon, Church of, 33
St. Thalelæus, 147
Suri, 64
Susanna, Monastery of, 148
Susiana, 111
Sycæ, 25, 134
Sycidaba, 113
Syria, 71, 72, 73
Syrtis the Lesser, 160, 161

T.

Tacapa, 160
Tanatas, 109
Tanaïs, River, 153
Taphosiris, 153
Taisus, 137
Tauri, 88
Tauroscythi, 88
Tauresium, 91
Telepta, 165
Tenedos, Island of, 128, 129
Tetrapyrgia, or the Four Towers, 91
Teuchria, 154
Thannurium, 57
Theodotus, Monastery of, 151
Thelphrache, Monastery of, 151
Thescus, 121
Theopolis, 68, 1^6, 151
Theodosiopolis, 3, 79, 81, 82, 83
Thermopylæ, 94, 95, 96, 97
Thessalonica, 99
Thebes, 97
Theodosiopolis, 47, 54, 57
Themeres, 57
Theodora, 110
Theodora, Baths of, 162
Theodoropolis, City, 113
Theodoropolis, Fort, 111
Thiolla, 57
Thrace, 89, 112, 114, 117, 119, 120
Tigas, 113
Tigris, River, 74
Tilicion, 114
Timena, 111
Toperus, 123
Trajanopolis, 122
Transmarisca, 113
Trapezus, 86, 87
Tripolis, 157, 159, 161
Tricattus, 97
Tricesa, Fort, 111
Tucca, 163
Tzanzakon, 86
Tzumina, 84

U.

Ulmiton, 114
Ulpiana, 92
Unnum, 96
Utos, 112

V.

Valeriana, 112
Variana, 112
Vernes, 109
Viminacium, 109
Virgin, at Porphyreon, House of the, 150

Virgin, at Jericho, Church of the, 147
Virgin, Church of the, 143
Virgin Mary, Church of, 15, 16, 26, 31

W.
Watchtower, 44

Z.
Zamarthas, 57
Zanes, 109
Zebinus, Monastery of, 151
Zenobia, 62, 63, 64
Zetnocortum, 112
Zeugma, 67
Zeuxippus, Baths of, 34

THE END.

Printed in Great Britain
by Amazon